D0639218

CRIES
Experiences

FOR PEACE

of Japanese Victims of World War II

compiled by
the Youth Division of Soka Gakkai

ROGERS LIBRARY
Maryknoll, N. Y. 10545

The **Japan Times**, Ltd.

940.548
So39

86-982

Copyrighted materials in this book are reproduced by permission as follows. The quotation of Arnold J. Toynbee from *Choose Life: A Dialogue Between Arnold Toynbee and Daisaku Ikeda,* by permission of the Oxford University Press; and from *The Toynbee-Ikeda Dialogue: Man Himself Must Choose,* by permission of Kodansha International. Li Po's "They Fought in the South," translated·by William McNaughton, and Pao Chao's "The Tedious Ways," translated by Jerome Ch'en and Michael Bullock, both from *Chinese Literature: An Anthology from the Earliest Times to the Present Day,* edited by William McNaughton, by permission of Charles E. Tuttle, Co. Alfred Hayes' "The Death of the Craneman" from *A New Anthology of Modern Poetry,* Random House, Modern Library, by permission of Alfred Hayes. George Barker's "Channel Crossing" from *Collected Poems by George Barker,* by permission of Faber and Faber, Ltd.

Edited by Richard L. Gage. Book design and typography by Rebecca M. Davis. Cover design by Nobu Miyazaki.

First English Edition, 1978

Published by The Japan Times, Ltd., 5-4 Shibaura 4-chome, Minato-ku, Tokyo 108, Japan. Copyright © 1974, 1975, 1976, 1978 by the Soka Gakkai Youth Division Antiwar Publication Committee; all rights reserved. Printed in Japan.

Contents

CONTENTS

WHAT WE HAVE DONE: Part 2   195

THE DANGER TODAY   235

Preface

NEVER TO EXPERIENCE WAR is to be blessed; not to understand how murderous and hideous war is invites the danger of plunging the world into the kind of global blood bath it has already endured twice in this century.

There are many young people today who have never experienced the fires and death of actual war. One way to ensure that they never do is to reveal to them the face of war unmasked in the hellish experiences of its victims. Such education is the goal of the efforts of the Youth Division of Soka Gakkai in compiling a set of fifty volumes of accounts of Japanese wartime suffering. The set has been published in Japanese under the title *Senso o shiranai sedai e* (To the Generations Who Do Not Know War). This volume, an English version of selected chapters from the full set, has been prepared under the auspices of the Soka Gakkai International Bureau, 32 Shinano-machi, Shinjuku-ku, Tokyo 160.

War is always inspired by holders of political power. No people wants to suffer in the way that armed conflict forces them to suffer. After the nightmarish experiences they underwent during World War II—especially the atomic bombings of Hiroshima and Nagasaki—the Japanese today are among the most peace-oriented people in the world. Indeed, their constitution renounces the right to belligerence as a means of settling international disputes.

Realizing that without knowledge error is likely, some of the Japanese victims of the war have agreed to write down their recollections in the hope that people everywhere will see what war does and strive to build lasting peace.

As all human suffering is similar, the experiences of these people resemble each other in broad outline. As each human being is unique, so each instance of human suffering has its own distinctive bitterness and lesson.

From the pages of this book you will hear the voices of some of the victims of World War II. The voices of countless others are now silenced forever. Let those who have survived cry out for all in a plea for peace. Let not all the blood have sunk wasted into the thirsty ground. Let not the pain have been for nothing. We must heed what the living sufferers—and through them the dead sufferers, as well—say. As one of the writers in this book suggests, we must try to make productive use of the horror. That use must take the form of lasting peace, for, armed as he is today, man has no alternative.

ISAO NOZAKI
DIRECTOR
YOUTH DIVISION
SOKA GAKKAI

WAR CAN BE ABOLISHED, even if it were to prove impossible to cure all human beings of committing nonmilitary crimes of violence. I think the invention of nuclear weapons makes it probable that we shall succeed in abolishing war, in spite of the difficulty of giving up a habit that is five thousand years old. The assumption underlying the institution of war was that one of the belligerents would win, that the other would lose, and that the advantage of victory for the winner would be greater than the cost. This calculation often proved wrong. Wars were often disastrous for the victors too. But it is clear that, in a war fought with nuclear weapons, there can be no such thing as even a costly victory. This prospect deprives states of a rational incentive for going to war.

However, human nature is only partially rational. It is conceivable that we might irrationally commit mass suicide.

ARNOLD J. TOYNBEE

CRIES FOR PEACE

CHAPTER ONE

What Good
Does This Do?

Crows, kites peck human bowels;
Carrying them, they fly
    and lay them on dead tree and branch.
Lieutenants, privates
    stain the grass and weeds.
Generals! Secretaries!
    what good does this do?
So we know:
    these so-called "arms"
        are really murderer's tools.
Benevolent men
    seek for them
        neither use nor excuse.

LI PO
"They Fought in the South"

When man wages war, each side of the conflict seeks to convince its supporters that any sacrifice is warranted. Killing, burning, pillaging — all acts condemned by humanity under circumstances of peace — become acceptable in the name of the cause of the moment, whatever it might be. Blindly accepting what their leaders say as true, large groups have committed mass suicide, mothers have abandoned their screaming infants, soldiers have turned weapons on their comrades. The cost for both winner and loser in spilled blood, broken bodies, destroyed property, and madness is so high that the sane man can only stand in amazement and ask himself, "What good does this do?"

Eight out of Twenty-five

Makato Ameku

RUMORS OF MASSIVE landings of United States troops had already been abroad for several days. At the time, I was living in an underground shelter in the village of Yomitanson. When the first American forces began arriving on April 1, 1945, villagers rushed to the shelter for refuge. The entire underground space was soon packed to the entrance. At about two o'clock in the morning, after the enemy had completed its operations, one of the leaders of the group in the shelter said, "It's far better to commit

17

suicide than to be killed by the enemy. Let's all die together."
The idea soon spread through the shelter. A man with battlefield
experience had a hand grenade. Though it might not be powerful
enough to kill all twenty-five of us, we decided to make an attempt.

After consideration, I too chose death. Together with me were
my mother-in-law and my husband's brothers and sisters. There
were five of us. My husband had gone to the Philippines shortly
after our marriage and had been missing ever since. I had a twen-
ty-year-old son, my sole hope in life; but he was in a field-
artillery unit rumored to have been destroyed in fierce daily
bombings by American planes. No word had reached me from
him since February. Without my son, I lacked both the courage
and desire to live any longer.

All twenty-five of us in the shelter arranged our personal
belongings and prepared for death. In the last few moments, I embraced my mother-in-law; but my thoughts were of my son. One
of my husband's younger sisters thanked me for having taken care
of her mother and the rest of the family even though my husband
had disappeared. She then said goodbye. My throat was so dry
that I could barely speak. I said that I wanted to tell everyone
goodbye, but someone beside me murmured, "The moment of
death is no time for talking."

Holding my mother-in-law close to me under the overcoat that
I had kept as a memento of my son, I already felt more dead than
alive. Then a man shouted at me, "Why are you wearing that
coat? The blast will kill you faster if you are unprotected." Re-
luctantly, I let the coat fall.

After a dreadful moment of silence, the leader shouted and
pulled the pin of the grenade. As the explosion ripped the air, I
covered my head again with my son's coat.

When I regained consciousness, I could not rise. I was lying on
the ground in a severe state of shock. My ears must have been
damaged; they were ringing. A thick cloud of dust and the stench
of gunpowder filled the shelter. My mind began to clear. I heard a

18

voice crying out, "I'm still alive!" Then there were groans of pain. I smelled something offensive that was not gunpowder. Close to my ears was a strange sound. Peering through the smoke, I saw that what I heard was the blood gurgling from the heart of a man who was still half alive. I do not want to recall any more.

Near dawn, guided by the late moonlight, I crept out through a crevice in the shelter wall. When I saw them shortly after daybreak, my clothes were dyed red with the blood of my mother-in-law. Only eight of the twenty-five of us survived.

Sinking of the Tsushima-maru
Sotoku Dana

In 1944, AFTER the crushing defeat suffered by the Japanese in Saipan, the government decided to evacuate women, children, and old people from Okinawa. At the time, I was a teacher in a fifth-grade class at the Tempi Higher Elementary School, in Naha. Because of the strong militaristic mood then prevailing all over the nation, children above the third grade were compelled to train their bodies and spirits by means of outdoor drills. In Okinawa, the sessions were held under a blazing sun. At first, some of the children suffered from sunstroke; but gradually they became accustomed to the regimen.

One of my school duties was to report on the progress of the war in the South Pacific by showing movements in as much detail as possible on a large map. Owing to this work, I had a greater knowledge of war strategy than my colleagues. On learning of the defeat in Saipan, I predicted that Okinawa would be attacked next for two reasons. First, the island was within the flying range of B-29s out of Saipan. Second, Okinawa was a vital strategic point between the Japanese main islands and the

South Pacific islands, where fierce fighting was still taking place.

Although the conditions of the militaristic society in which we lived prevented me from talking about it with anyone but a few of my most intimate friends, I realized that if attacked Okinawa would be destroyed and that all thought of further educational activities would be out of the question. The children would have to be evacuated, and I decided to join the first evacuation group as a chaperon.

On September 18, three nine-thousand-ton ships were waiting at Naha port to evacuate about five hundred children and thirty teachers from five elementary schools in Naha, plus children and adults from other parts of Okinawa. Parents carried food and clothing to the ships, which had earlier been used to transport troops from Manchuria to Okinawa.

The ship called the Tsushima-maru, which we boarded, had two holds, one forward and one aft. The Naha group was assigned to the forward hold, and the children and adults from other parts of the island to the aft hold. We left Naha at dusk, as the sun was about to set behind the Kerama island chain. The three transport ships formed a triangle, flanked by two destroyers. The Tsushima-maru was on the left side of the convoy.

Because enemy submarines were thought to be more active in the evening and morning, we anchored overnight between Sesoko Island and Motobu, on Okinawa. The next morning we set sail for Miyazaki, on Kyushu.

All the children were in high spirits. Accompanied by thirty teachers and assured time and time again that Japan would never be defeated, they acted as if they were going on a picnic. Firm faith in the deterrent powers of the destroyers sailing with us encouraged the adults as well. No one seemed very concerned.

The young army officer in charge of the evacuation, however, reminded me of the danger of enemy submarines and asked me to keep the children calm and off the decks. Any carelessness — for instance a bit of wastepaper thrown overboard — could inform

20

enemy submarines of our presence. As leader of the group, I was responsible for taking these instructions to the others.

The blackout imposed in the holds made it impossible for me to see anyone except the children immediately under the sole light permitted to us. Because I had no microphone, I had to shout. Soon, I was very hoarse. For two days we remained in the dark, hot hold. The faster vessels in the convoy adjusted their speed to the slower ones as we sailed on.

On the morning of September 22, the commanding officer called me to his cabin and informed me that enemy submarines now surrounded us. The extreme danger of our situation required complete quiet from the children. But in spite of my warnings, many of them continued to play noisily. Later on the same day, the commanding officer ordered me and all other teachers to remain awake all night. At the time, we were between the island Amami Oshima and Kagoshima, on Kyushu. We were near the Sea of Shichito, where high waves and numerous tiny islands made sea traveling perilous.

On board our ship was a large number of bamboo rafts that had been provided for the troop transfer from Manchuria. Each raft could carry five or six people. On the day we received the order to remain awake all night, we were further instructed to bring the rafts on deck. Looking at scores of them stacked there, I felt my confidence in the destroyers begin to fail.

Our next instructions were to bring the children on the deck and have them practice climbing the long rope-ladders that provided emergency escape from the deep holds. The older children, who probably sensed increasing danger, took our instructions seriously and cooperated. But the very young, already tired and seasick, refused to do as they were told and seemed oblivious to what was happening. Soon the decks were so crowded with children that there was no place to lie down. Returning to the dark hold, I found some children remaining there. Although I could not identify them, I assumed they were younger children

21

who had come back to the hold when they saw how crowded the decks were.

After my trip to the hold, I began inquiring after one of my colleagues, who had brought seven members of his family with him. It turned out that they had all gone to the doctor's cabin, since one of them was suffering from acute pneumonia. Ascertaining this, I began thinking of my own mother, wife, and daughter — a first-grade pupil — who were on the ship, too. I found them in the hold and took them to the deck, where I sought out a very small place for them to sit. Then I found a tiny place next to the side of the ship for myself. As I sat leaning against the side, I thought about my responsibilities. Although there were still children in the hold, against orders, there was nothing I could do about it. Again and again, I said to myself, "It can't be helped. I've done all I can."

Several of the soldiers who had been standing at a cannon in the bow came over to talk with me. One of them said, "This ship is lucky. On the way to Okinawa from Manchuria, she was hit by a torpedo. But it didn't explode."

At about ten in the evening, when all the children were sound asleep and when I had begun to nod in the perfect calm, a thunderous sound came from the opposite side of the ship. The hold where we had been only a few hours earlier had sustained a direct hit. In a few seconds, I felt things falling on me; but I was dazed and shocked. I did not know what the things were. As my mind began to clear slowly, I saw that only fifty or sixty centimeters in front of me everything had been blown away. On the very spot where there was now a gaping chasm, minutes ago small children had slept on a cloth spread for them. Sea water roared in from a hole blasted in the side of the ship.

I was confused and did not know what to do until one of the soldiers that I had been talking with earlier shouted, "Quick! Go to the upper deck!" When I arrived there, I saw three children who had been blown upward from below by the explosion. One

22

of the soldiers said, "They are dead. There's nothing we can do for them." Suddenly my mind was completely clear.

Until that second, ever since the moment of the explosion, I had thought only of escape. I completely forgot my responsibilities as a teacher. I had been about to jump into the sea with my daughter in my arms. But when I saw the bodies of those dead children, I knew my duty.

Asking my wife to watch our daughter, I went down into the hold, which was rapidly filling with water. The rope ladders had been destroyed; and as I hurried down the twisted steel staircase, for the first time I realized that my legs were full of shrapnel. In the dark, swirling, watery hell of the hold, children screamed for aid. But I was powerless to help them.

The stern of the ship began to sink as the prow heaved upward. Under the pressure of sea water, the hull began to collapse with a terrible sound. I saw that it was too late to do anything for the people in the hold. Hurrying to the deck, where I was lucky enough to find my wife and daughter quickly, I said that we must jump into the sea, as some of the soldiers had already started doing. The prow was very high, because the ship was rapidly sinking. My wife said a jump from such a height would be fatal. But we had little time to think about it, for we were all suddenly hurled overboard.

I surfaced only instants before I would have drowned. I was saved because my little finger accidentally hooked in the strap of my daughter's life jacket. Since she was very small, the buoyancy of the adult life jacket she wore was sufficient to pull us both to the surface. If this had not happened, the raging waters stirred up by the sinking ship would have kept me under water so long that I would have died. When the two of us surfaced, I found that my daughter was alive, though she seemed to have swallowed some sea water.

By this time, the ship had sunk. Oddly, I was composed enough to give thought to what we ought to do to survive. My

23

daughter clung to my back, and I wrapped my arm around a floating log. Soon I saw a capsized boat not far away. When the order had come to abandon ship, children near the boat had boarded it. But the whirlpool caused by the sinking ship had turned it over, trapping fifty or sixty children inside. I learned this from a teacher who managed to escape from the capsized boat.

I found a small place at the bow; but it was sloping, and the waves made it impossible for me to get on, though I tried several times. Then an empty bamboo raft drifted close. I asked a young man nearby to watch my daughter and swam to the raft. When I had pulled it to the capsized boat, the young man, my daughter, and I boarded it. As we floated along, we saw many people clinging to bits of debris. Summoning up my flagging strength, I called to them, "Cheer up. Rescue is bound to come in the morning."

We heard children crying our names from various directions. Ten of them swam to our raft and got on, but their weight sank it; and they were forced to cling to whatever they found floating.

After a while, I saw my wife clutching a log. When she drew near, I pulled her onto our raft. In the faint light ahead we could see an island, Akuseki of the Satsunan group. The current seemed to branch to left and right as it approached the island. The lighter floating objects with people clinging to them were being carried to the right; our heavier raft was being carried to the left. For a while many of us were together. We called to encourage each other. But by the dawn of September 23, all the children in our vicinity had floated out of sight. The two currents did not move at the same speed.

At about nine in the morning, a Japanese plane circled above us. The pilot waved a handkerchief; and we waved back, confident that rescue would come soon. But it did not, and we began seven days of drifting without food or water.

On our raft were my wife, my daughter, and I; the young man from the capsized boat; a soldier; and an old man we picked up early in the course of our drifting. On the second night, the young man said goodbye and jumped into the sea. We later learned that he had probably fallen victim to the hallucinations a person may experience under conditions of extreme exhaustion.

Though the raft supported us, we were waist deep in water and had to hang on very tight to prevent being washed away by the waves. In the daytime, it was burning hot; at night, it was bitterly cold.

On the third night, my daughter began to complain. She wanted to go home. She wanted water. My heart ached because I could do nothing for her. At about midnight, my wife, who had been holding her, said that our child had stopped moving. I took her in my arms. With her last strength she clung to my neck and then died of cold and exposure. I could not bring myself to set her body adrift. I tied her to the raft, saying to myself that we would all be dead before long.

On the fourth day, the old man jumped into the sea. I pulled him back to the raft. But in a period of hours, he jumped in again so often that finally I let him stay in the water. Then, suddenly, he screamed, "Poisonous snake!" Quickly we dragged him onto the raft only to see that a shark had torn a huge strip of flesh from his left buttock and side. The wound was so large that we were unable to stop the bleeding. Soon he died from loss of blood. Clasping our hands in prayer for the repose of his soul, we set his body adrift.

Our raft continued to ride on waves that reached heights of seven or eight meters. We later learned that heavy seas in the region into which we had drifted had prevented fishing boats from rescuing us. Rafts and people that had drifted in the opposite direction were rescued within a few days after the sinking of the ship. Each evening, we thought we would die in the night. Each morning, we wondered if we would live to sunset.

On the seventh day, I learned the nature of the hallucinations the young man and the old man had suffered. I experienced them too. Once I saw myself and a group of students from Naha undergoing outdoor drill at a place called Katabaru. I pinched myself to find out if I was asleep. Because I felt the pain, I was convinced that the illusion was the truth and that I could get water at the camp site. I had begun to walk toward the place when my wife's scream brought me back to the raft. In another instance, I saw the two of us and our raft in front of the public hall in Naha. I told my wife that we would be able to get off and go home. She replied that she could not see the public hall. I pinched myself again. My mind was working. It was extreme fatigue that made my nerves conjure up these illusions. Later, an elderly couple told how the ten children who had been on their raft, one by one had said, "Well, here we are at home," and jumped into the sea.

Soon, however, my illusions vanished. The shores of the island Amami Oshima came into sight. At about ten in the morning on the eighth day, we drifted into an inlet with a mountain straight ahead and rock cliffs on both sides.

The tide was at ebb. As we drew closer to land, we saw a spring of water in the cliff. The soldier swam in to drink. At that time, waves were lapping the sandy shore; but at flood tide, they would crash against the cliff walls. I left the raft and walked shoreward. I was too weak to carry my daughter's body, but the waves brought her to me. My wife remained on the raft. I told her to stay there until the tide raised her to a place where she could get off on a boulder. She was extremely weak but, after several attempts, managed to land. Unable to move, she lay down on the sunbaked rocks.

I hurried to the spring and drank as much water as I could hold. When I recovered from the first frenzy of drinking, I tried to carry water to my wife. She was only ten meters away, but I stumbled and trembled so badly that I could not carry water to her in my hands. The soldier took off the *senninbari* * cloth sash he wore. We wrung it as dry as possible and then soaked it in fresh water and took it to her.

---

* *Senninbari* sashes were covered with a thousand stitches made by a thousand women (*senninbari*) and were given as talismans to soldiers going into battle.

26

We had at last quenched our thirst but now found ourselves surrounded by cliffs and a mountain and the rising tide. The soldier said, "It looks like we've made it this far only to die here." "Don't talk like a fool!" I shouted. "We've got to climb the cliff." The two of us did. We left my wife on the beach, promising to come for her as soon as possible. It took six hours to reach the top. Miraculously, neither of us slipped. It was night when we lay down in the grass field that crowned the cliff.

On the following day we walked until at last we found first a cultivated rice paddy — a sign of human habitation — and then a village. A young man rushed to us, asked if we were schoolteachers from the wrecked ship, and informed us that a squad of thirty fire fighters was ready to move into rescue action at once. I did not know exactly where we had left my wife, but I described the place to the best of my ability. The rescue squad departed and returned with her in about an hour. Two girls and three women who had been rescued by fishing boats two days before had been brought to the same village.

We were given tea and sugar-water and told to rest for a few hours before moving on to the naval port of Koniya. All survivors were ordered to go there because the navy wished to keep the sinking of the ship a secret.

After a short rest, I asked for pencil and paper and wrote a detailed report of the sinking of the ship and the way in which we had been set adrift. I asked the captain of a submarine to carry the letter to the principal of my school in Naha. In it, I said that I hoped to return to Naha as quickly as possible; but the principal replied later with a request that I go on to Miyazaki and remain there to care for other children to be evacuated on other ships. Accordingly, I went to Miyazaki, where I stayed for two years before returning at last to Naha.

Because I had been able to do nothing to save many children from agonizing suffering and death, I felt disqualified to serve further as a teacher. I decided to work at sea for the rest of my life, for, in doing so, I hoped to do even a little to calm the souls of my

27

daughter; my mother, who was never seen by any of us after the sinking; and all the children who perished in the disaster. A year after returning to Naha, I took a job with a fishery.

No Matter What Happens, Live!

Toyoko Azama

BEFORE HIS DEATH of illness, in 1943, my father had amassed enough money in the business of catching and processing bonito on the island of Tokashiki, west of Okinawa, to provide for all of us. We lived in a spacious house in the center of our village, just across from the local school.

On September 10, 1944, Japanese troops under the command of a Captain Tamura landed on our island and requisitioned our house as their headquarters. We had to live in some of the small back rooms.

On October 10, planes circled over the village. Mistaking them for Japanese craft, the soldiers in our house climbed onto the roof and waved flags. In fact, they were American reconnaissance planes. They soon left, but in their wake came fighters and bombers. The ensuing raid destroyed all the fishing boats on the island, including, of course, those belonging to our family. The enemy probably considered our house an especially important building, since on its roof were large black letters saying "Headquarters of the Tamura Company."

After their first raids, the Americans flew over so often that all of us were ordered to work in the fields only at night or very early in the morning. In the daytime we had air-raid drills and helped in the construction of shelters for the Japanese forces by carrying gravel and rocks in bamboo baskets or by laying turf. School classes were held no more than two or three hours a day. Some of the shelters we built were for suicide boats stationed at a nearby village. A large number of Korean laborers was engaged in this operation.

The war situation continued to worsen and reached a peak of danger on March 23, 1945, when bombing attacks and incendiary bombs destroyed many houses — including ours — and the school building. Soldiers and civilians alike hid in the large, turf-covered shelter dug under the school playground. Then on the morning of March 24, the liaison officer of the home-defense unit told us to evacuate to Mount Nishi. Though we all thought the shelter safe, we did as instructed, since the officers told us the enemy was planning a landing on our island. By twos and threes, the villagers came out of the shelter and started on the long walk. The men carried sickles, hoes, and hatchets for building shelters on the mountain; and the women bore bundles of foodstuffs on their heads.

Staying off the road, we waded through a stream in a narrow ravine. The current of the swollen river made walking difficult. It was dark, and a torrential, ominous rain drenched us to the skin.

Families stayed in groups, the younger and stronger carrying infants and assisting the infirm. Mother carried my young brother, and I led my younger sister by the hand. We tried to encourage each other as much as possible and to forget our weariness. Limp as rags, we rested briefly after dawn and then climbed the mountain.

The village headman and a policeman, who were among our party, held a conference with other leaders and examined the coastline with binoculars, trying to estimate the chances the Japanese troops would have of fighting off the enemy. Shortly after the meeting of leaders ended, families began to assemble in groups and to whisper among themselves in a strange way.

The headman addressed us all. "Enemy warships surround our island. The situation for us is hopeless. If we live, the Americans will capture us and gouge out our eyes and cut off our noses. Let us die together, honorably, with a prayer for the eventual victory of our empire."

At first, there was a great commotion among the four hundred villagers and members of the home guard gathered there. (There were no Japanese soldiers among us.) Then everyone grew quiet. Sakè bottles were passed around for final farewell toasts.

The policeman gave out hand grenades and instructed us in their use. Then, standing at attention, we all shouted, "Long live the emperor!" three times. One after another, the people with grenades pulled the pins. Screams mingled with the roar of the explosions. Many people were blown to pieces; others, maimed but still alive, groaned in agony.

Our family sat on the ground in a circle, my uncle in the middle with the hand grenade. A few seconds after he pulled the pin, there was a tremendous explosion. I closed my eyes but remained conscious. When I furtively opened my eyes, I saw my uncle lying on his side. The hand in which he had held the grenade was upraised, like a crimson flower of skinless, fleshless bones. The head was blown from the body of the two-year-old baby my aunt had held in her arms. Three fingers were blown from her hand that had cradled the infant's head. My sister-in-law, her sister, and her two children had died without making a sound. Though my uncle was seriously hurt, none of my immediate family had died.

Several people had been spared death because their hand grenades had not gone off. Those of us who could walk started down the mountain but were stopped by a large group of villagers from Aharen. These people told us that the enemy was waiting in the foothills to torture or kill us. They told us we would do better to return to the mountain and commit suicide.

We returned to see people trying to kill themselves with hoes or whatever they had. One man systematically hacked his family to death with a hatchet. A young mother killed each of her children, all of whom sat silent and unresisting. The same woman, noticing that my uncle was still alive, killed him with a hatchet. The Aharen villagers, too, had started committing suicide. A middle-aged woman thrust a hoe into the belly of her daughter-in-law. Blood and entrails spilled out.

Screams of suffering mingled with the cries of those who did not want to die. My younger sister shrieked that she wanted to run away. But I held her hand tightly and made her lie down. I lay on top of her to keep her from wriggling free. Men were walking about clubbing people who were still alive. My sister continued to struggle, causing me to move slightly. I heard a voice say, "This one's still alive," and then felt a blow crushing my head. I later learned that the person who struck me was a young man from our village. I knew him.

I came to after a while and, with a still fuzzy mind, heard cries. "Please spare me." "Please help me." "Please kill me."

My mother was alive but injured. With one hand she held her head; her skull had been cracked by a club blow. With the other hand she held my young brother, who had fainted. The blow dealt him had caused his face to swell and contort; he was foaming at the mouth. My younger sister was unharmed.

The dead were lucky. The maimed and injured suffered indescribably. Some people hanged themselves from the trees. A doctor from the village sat in the center of his family. He had pulled the pin, but the grenade had not gone off. "Don't we have a weapon of some kind?" he asked. His son offered a folding knife. "Then we'll begin with Mother," said the doctor, as he severed her carotid artery. She fell with a quiet moan. One by one, the doctor killed his family, then bound the knife between two branches, climbed the tree, and fell so that the blade penetrated his throat, killing him in a few minutes.

Mother, who had bandaged her head with a wrapping cloth, said we had to do something about brother, who was still unconscious and frothing at the mouth. According to an old wives' tale, the smell of earth could revive wounded people. I held a handful of it to his nose without effect. Mother then suggested we

31

pour water over him. I found a jug, went to a nearby stream, and filled it with bloody water. Soon after I poured it over my brother, he regained consciousness, though his eyes were still bleary and he still frothed. I continued to hold earth to his nostrils.

In the gathering twilight, the half dead, disheveled hair straggling over their shoulders, began to wander among the corpses. We no longer had any business among the dead and, after discussing the matter with the survivors, we decided to descend the mountain.

Seven of us — mother, brother, sister, and I, and three women from Aharen — headed toward the ravine that we had followed in our ascent but made a mistake and ended up on the coast where American warships were pounding the island. Scared out of our wits, we hurried to take shelter behind some boulders on the mountainside. Six females and a small boy, we were without protection and provisions. All I had in my satchel was the schoolbooks I had kept with me throughout flight and life in the shelter.

After dark, we resumed our descent, this time along the right ravine. My brother had regained a certain amount of strength. I carried him on my back, while mother led my small sister. We could not see clearly and had to grope our way, clutching at trees and bushes. Once I reached for support and grabbed the legs of a hanged man. My heart nearly stopped beating with shock and horror. Looking about me, I dimly saw eight rigid corpses dangling from the trees. I still shudder when I recall them.

After dawn, we hid behind boulders. Before long, we heard automobiles. Peeping out, we saw some very tall, white-robed Americans go into the mountains. What could they be doing? They emerged shortly, bearing on stretchers people who had been wounded in the mass suicide. Mother said it was bad that the Americans had penetrated this far. They could easily catch and kill us. She put her hand over my brother's mouth to quiet his whimpering.

We hid all day and, at night, started down the mountain but got lost again. Retracing our steps, we found a cave, where we hid. Footsteps outside startled us, but it was only a member of the home guard. This kind man gave us what information he could and showed us the way down. Parting from us, he said, "No matter what happens, live! Never think of killing yourselves again."

During the night, a man wounded in the chest climbed to a place near our cave and killed his wife and children, who had been hiding there. Mad from pain and from grief over what he had done, he lurched into a stream, where he stood shouting for water. My mother scooped up some of the water in which he waded, and he drank from her hands. There was a handkerchief stuffed in the bullet hole in his chest. For a while, he babbled madly, then he seemed to regain sanity. He told us the way to the evacuation point where other villagers were hiding. We set out at once.

In reaching the shelter, we saw many American emplacements and foxholes, but no Americans. It was still dark. I later learned that the Americans took their battle positions by day and retired to their ships at night to avoid Japanese attacks. In the emplacements we found canned food, cheese, and candy. Mother told me not to touch them: they might be poisoned. But one of the women from Aharen said, "Eat them; they're good." All we had tasted for days was a small amount of raw rice and some dried fish washed down with the disgusting bloody water of the stream. I ate some of the American candy.

It was daylight already. We found a clear stream and scooped up drinking water in a can. Then we rested for a while. Suddenly we heard an automobile and voices talking in English. All seven of us dashed into a bamboo groove before the Americans reached the stream. They found the can and noticed wet footprints on the flat rocks where we had stood. From our hiding place, we could see them; but though they searched, they did not find us. After a while, they gave up and went away.

After dusk, we sneaked past the American positions, crossed the valley, and hurried toward our destination.

Out of the dark, we saw the beam of a flashlight hit a boulder.

We flew for cover behind a tree. Then a voice called in Japanese, "Who's there? Islanders?"

With a sigh of relief, we identified ourselves and said where we were going. The man, Captain Suzuki of the communications company stationed on our island, was an acquaintance. He was happy to see that we had survived. Word of the mass suicide on Mount Nishi had already reached him. Counseling us not to go on that night because of the late hour, he offered us the beds he had made by spreading folded tents on the ground. We gladly accepted his kind hospitality. As we slept, he sat near us, his sword held upright between his legs and his head leaning against it. Soldiers patrolled the place all night.

The following morning, the captain had some of his men escort us to the evacuation point, where about forty villagers expressed their happiness that we had been spared. All of them were wounded, and the heat made their wounds fester and stink very fast. The serious injury to my mother's head had already reached a grave state. I had to hold a handkerchief over my nose to keep from being overcome by the odor.

The lack of food and the crowded conditions soon convinced mother and me that we ought to leave for the home of my uncle who had been killed in the mass suicide. It was a strong, well-built house in a sheltered place. We lived there till the end of June. Each day, since I was the only one old and fit enough for the task, I went foraging for whatever vegetables I could find. In the ruins of a storehouse, I found some unburned rice, which I scraped from the ground and took home. It was a very valuable acquisition for us. Japanese medics administered treatment to the wounded once a week. Thanks to them, my mother's head healed before too long. But food continued to be a serious problem for everyone. Even the Japanese soldiers were forced to beg like paupers.

One day, a certain Corporal Takahashi, who had taught me songs and helped me with difficult arithmetic problems when we were still living in my family's home, came to see us. I was fond of him. In a way, he had taken my father's place. He brought us a bag of dried bread and the sad news that he had come to say farewell. He had been given a dangerous reconnaissance mission. After a brief chat, he departed. Four hours later, I saw soldiers carrying his body, riddled with six bullet holes, cold, dead, past our door.

As all other food ran out, the islanders began butchering their few cows and pigs. They shared with relatives but with no one else. Mother had come from Okinawa and had no relatives on the island, and father was dead. That meant we were offered none of this important food. But mother had a bright idea. She said to me, "Go to the stream where they butcher. You'll probably find the entrails there. Wash them and bring them home." I did as she told me. We cooked the entrails with garlic, and they helped us to survive and to maintain a degree of health.

One of my schoolteachers, who had been drafted into the home guard, came back to the village to see his family. His wife, who had just given birth to their fifth child, was living with their children in an air-raid shelter. Though he was supposed to return to duty at once, he stayed on in the village out of concern for his family's welfare. A few days passed; then Japanese soldiers came and took him away. "Who's more important: the emperor or your family?" they asked him.

Later the teacher's wife and children went to the army barracks but were not allowed in. It turned out that the Japanese soldiers had executed the man.

After June, violent battles between the Japanese and the Americans made my uncle's home no longer safe. We went to a cave shelter that belonged to a friend of my father. There we found a bushel of rice, some unrefined sugar, and several pieces of dried bonito. This kept us alive for a while; but soon I had to resume the search for food, a search that was both arduous and dangerous. On several occasions I was nearly shot trying to fetch water from streams or salt water from the sea. We were ultimately reduced to eating starch prepared by allowing the pith of the

Japanese sago palm to rot. Lack of salt and vegetables resulted in frequent cases of beriberi.

Early in August, American troops appealed through loud-speakers for us to come out. The war was over, they said. From planes they dropped leaflets urging the islanders to come out of mountain shelters. Many of the villagers reacted promptly and came out in large groups, waving white flags improvised from towels, wrapping cloths, and even men's loincloths.

We were wondering what to do, when some Japanese soldiers came to us and said, "If you surrender, we'll execute you as spies." Ten of these soldiers kept constant guard over eight families — including ours — and did not permit us to surrender.

One night we heard shots in the brush outside the shelter. Three old men who had given themselves up had returned to collect some of their property. They told the villagers being held by the Japanese that the Americans did them no harm and gave them food. Only one of these old men managed to return to the Americans. The Japanese soldiers shot the other two.

Finally, however, the soldiers received word from imperial headquarters that the war was over and joined us in giving ourselves up. On the site of our old house, the Americans sprayed us white with DDT and gave us clean clothes.

We cooked in cans with wire handles. Groups of four or five children polished American soldiers' shoes in exchange for food. After a while, we all took part in various rehabilitation projects. A tent school was set up; a distribution center for rationed foods was established. Villagers who had come out of hiding earlier were already building huts and barracks with whatever materials they could collect. All we had was a tent the Americans gave us. We set it up on the land where our house had stood. We had lost everything in the war and, with no man to help us, had to rely on relief.

Some time after the end of the war, the wife of our schoolteacher got permission to look for the remains of her husband. My mother and I helped her. People who had witnessed the execution told us where he was buried. We found the skeleton of his torso and limbs. No head. Then, not far away, we uncovered a severed head and neck. Around the neck was twisted a rusted piece of wire.

Lost Years of Youth
Fumiko Nakane

OUR PLAN TO ESCAPE from Americans landing on Okinawa failed. My mother and I had assumed they would land on the side of the island facing the East China Sea and therefore fled to the Pacific side. The Americans landed on the Pacific side.

Soon I was separated from my mother because I was inducted into the Ryukyu Unit as a field nurse. Only sixteen, I was the youngest and the smallest of our group of eighteen nurses. My uniform was baggy, and my shoes heavy and cumbersome. I was ordered to carry a mine to the battlefield. It was heavy. I stumbled and fell often. My comrades helped me to stand each time, but I cried and called for my mother so frequently that my superiors scolded me harshly. They tried to encourage me by promising that after my death I would be enshrined in the Yasukuni Shrine, in Tokyo, where Japanese military war-dead are commemorated. Because of the militaristic indoctrination we had all received this did actually cheer me somewhat.

After successfully completing this first dangerous mission, we headed for the field hospital at Kanegusuku, nursing the wounded we encountered on the way. In the heat, wounds festered and became infested with maggots in two or three hours. One of the wounded men asked me several times for tomatoes. Hoping to do what I could to ease his pain, I went out in the dark of night to try to find some in a neighboring field. Fumbling about, I stepped on

37

something soft. I saw at once that it was one of the many decayed and decaying corpses lying all around. Controlling my fear and horror, I finally located some tomatoes. They were a splendid kind that no one would expect to find in a scorched battlefield. I took them back to the wounded man as fast as I could.

Naval gunfire from the American ships off the coast intensified and took the life of my elder sister — among countless others. According to the story I heard later from her mother-in-law, my sister had been nursing her infant child under a tree. Suddenly the baby screamed. My sister's mother-in-law turned quickly to see my sister, headless but still holding to her breast her infant, now bathed in blood gushing from the stump of the mother's neck. My sister was buried without a head.

Many people were buried in the very craters where American naval bombardments had killed them, only to be exhumed when other shells landed in the same place. Soon there was nowhere to lay the dead.

Though we arrived at the field hospital in Kanegusuku, we were not admitted, because we were not full-fledged nurses. We had to take cover in shelters dug by local civilians. While there, we slept in circles to protect ourselves from Japanese soldiers.

The enemy surrounded the Japanese forces. But we soon heard the glad news that reinforcements from the mainland were due to come to our rescue on June 15. We prepared festive food and waited for their arrival. They never came.

Soon Kanegusuku fell under such heavy attacks that we had to evacuate to Mabuni. I noticed people giving injured personnel injections as we got ready to leave. At first, I assumed that the fluid was some kind of tonic to help the injured withstand the journey. I later learned that it was poison. People unable to walk were killed. I resolved then and there to do all I could to avoid injury.

At Mabuni, we learned that enemy attacks there were so severe that we had to pull back to a village called Maezato. The leader of my unit entrusted me with important documents stored in wicker cases together with some kerosene with which to burn them should they be in danger of falling into enemy hands. Everyone left, except two wounded soldiers and four nurses. Then three of the nurses joined their families, leaving me alone with the men. I resolved to find my mother as quickly as I could. Burning the important documents, I located my mother; and the two of us hastened to a nearby shelter. Americans soon came and forced us into the open. Some of them whistled and made gestures at us. As a proud member of the Ryukyu Unit, I was insulted by their behavior and started to fire at them with a pistol I was still carrying. My mother stopped me by warning that such an action on my part might imperil all the other people in the shelter. Outside, we were herded together. It was dark. Having heard that their blue eyes made Americans night blind, I tried to run away but at once learned that the rumor about them was false. Armed men surrounded us. Most of the men in our group had been shot.

For three days we were kept in a camp surrounded by barbed wire. It rained, and we had no roof over our heads. Though the Americans gave us food, we would not eat it because we thought it was poisoned.

When three days had passed, we were loaded on a boat, just south of Itoman. Convinced that the Americans were about to kill us, my mother and I ripped bands of cloth from our cotton trousers and tied our hands and feet together so that we would die in a decent posture.

But we reached the Chatan coast safely. There are large caves and pits in the ground on that part of the island. Believing this to be the place where they were going to bury us, we all trembled with fear. But once again, our fears were unfounded. The Americans loaded us onto trucks and took us to a detention camp in Kamara, in the central part of Okinawa. For a long time, however, we suffered in uncertainty.

During the fighting on Okinawa, ugliness among supposed friends was not uncommon. The Japanese soldiers often forced Okinawans from shelters into the open, where they were gunned down by the enemy. Japanese officers turned their swords on

Okinawans who would not leave shelters without an argument. I once witnessed Japanese soldiers torturing a sixteen-year-old Okinawan girl for being a spy. They tied her to a tree and did the most horrible things to her. When she fainted, they poured water over her head to revive her before beginning to torture her again. She was being punished this way because she had been found with one of the leaflets dropped by the American planes. The leaflets read, "Japan is going to lose the war anyway. Surrender now." The poor girl died for having this piece of paper.

I was the only one of the eighteen nurses in our group to survive. The Japanese government enshrined the war dead in Yasukuni Shrine, but no one has ever apologized to us for what we suffered or for the years of our youth that were stolen from us.

The Travels of War
Matsushi Shimabukuro

AT THE AGE OF TWENTY-THREE, I was forced to leave my beautiful village south of Nago, Okinawa, and join the Japanese army. In 1938, the unit of the Sixth Division to which I was assigned disembarked, under the cover of darkness, in China, somewhere on the coast of the Yellow Sea. We spent the night in vacant houses and the next day began a forced march to northern China. Under a blazing sun over a seemingly boundless stretch of flat plain, we trudged along fully armed and burdened with all our baggage. Because the Japanese occupied most of China at the time, we saw Chinese only at certain places. Chinese girls sometimes approached us with insinuating smiles. They wanted to exchange their favors for supplies.

Though exhausted by the long march and apprehensive about the battles that lay ahead, I was ready to do what I considered my duty. Militarism was deeply etched in my mind and in the minds of my friends. During the march my comrades and I often talked about our determination to fight to the best of our ability. We had come to die for the emperor. Since we were his, such a death was the highest possible honor. During military training we had constantly heard our instructors say, "Once you're on enemy territory, be prepared to die an honorable death. Do not be afraid of combat and do not come back home alive." But when we reached our destination, we learned that we were unwanted and returned at once to divisional headquarters in Kumamoto, on Kyushu. I was discharged from the military and allowed to return to my home on Okinawa.

Then the Pacific War began with the surprise Japanese attack on Pearl Harbor. For a while, the Japanese captured one important position after another; but in 1942, the Allies mounted a counteroffensive. At about this time, I served as a draftee in constructing an airfield on the island of Ieshima. Explosives were used to level the rugged terrain for the project. Since the construction officials did not take adequate safety precautions to protect the Okinawan laborers, accidents were frequent. One young man of barely twenty was killed when a flying stone struck him in the head. I was allowed to go home once but had to return to make up the labor quota required of our village. Throughout the period of hard work I spent there, we had to haul water from a remote village because there was none in the vicinity of the site.

When the war situation grew increasingly grave for Japan, the military forces began preparations for what was to be the decisive battle of Okinawa. The entire civilian population of the Ryukyu Islands was mobilized for the construction of subterranean shelters and emplacements. I was recalled into the army and assigned to a unit deployed around Shuri, where the head command of Japanese army forces on Okinawa was located.

On April 1, 1945, American troops landed on the beaches of Okinawa and, owing to their superior weaponry, advanced southward at a terrific speed. American ships virtually filling the seas

41

provided constant support for ground action by means of intense bombardment and raids from carrier-based planes. Bombing, strafing, and rocketing ripped open the mountains and fields and shook the very earth.

The Japanese had the advantage of knowledge of the peculiar terrain and made good use of it to unleash heavy artillery fire from concealed positions in caves, emplacements, natural escarpments, and terraces. They further employed desperation in the form of human bullets—men, carrying explosives, who threw themselves at American units.

I was in charge of a group of new conscripts and members of the Okinawa home guard. Since their duty was mainly to transport ammunition and supplies, they were armed with nothing but bamboo spears. They had no chance against the well-equipped American units with which they sometimes came into contact. Most of them were teen-agers. What weapons were given to new conscripts were far from satisfactory. Their grenade dischargers, for instance, were effective only at a limited range. Nothing with which we were armed could withstand the American tanks. Still, some young men tied explosives to their backs and dashed against the steel flanks of these onrushing vehicles. Many of them were no more than nineteen or twenty and had the faces of children.

The battling around Shuri lasted for about two months. During that time, fierce Japanese resistance checked American advances to the south. But the cost was murderous for both sides. Sometimes hundreds of men would die on a single day, and the fields were virtually dyed red with their blood.

The continual rains of May and June flooded our shelters, covered everything with mud, and intensified the misery of soldiers already hungry, dirty, and ragged. In our cave, mud had almost entirely blocked the entrance and exit by the time we were finally ordered to retreat, in the first week of June. We dug our way out. But outside, retreat was hazardous because the American fleet continued to bombard the Shuri defense line. We saw that there was an interval of about ten meters between the points at which naval shells landed. This gap enabled us to escape the area. There was only a handful of us by this time, since most of the new conscripts and members of the home guard had already been killed. One of my comrades and I set out together on either the fifth or sixth of June. I had been in fierce combat for so long that I had no clear idea of the date.

The forest that had once stood around our cave was gone; not a single tree remained. The city of Shuri was destroyed. Only rubble and charred stumps remained of the high coral-block walls and magnificent pine trees of ancient Shuri Castle. The stench of rotting human flesh hung over a field of desolation. Inside the castle area were many American soldiers. My comrade and I managed to dart past the battered ramparts and crumbled stone gate and run to a nearby millet field and then toward a large tomb in the Shikina Cemetery. Perhaps the millet waved suspiciously as we passed through it. Something must have given us away, for the Americans in the castle ruins fired but missed us. After tremendous effort, we managed to reach a blasted Japanese army storehouse near the Ichinichi Bridge. We found some scattered uniforms, which we quickly exchanged for our ragged ones.

After a while, we came to two or three houses that had escaped damage. They were surrounded by trees. As we drew nearer, a woman stepped from one of the houses, caught sight of us, and hurriedly tried to reenter. I called to her in the Okinawan dialect, and she returned. She had tried to flee because she thought we were Japanese. She said, "The Japanese soldiers are bad; they take away our food." Relieved to learn that we were Okinawans, she kindly gave us a basket of the sweet potatoes she had just dug and steamed. We ate all we could and put the rest in our pockets. Then we went into one of the unoccupied houses, where we found salt and lard to rub on wounds we had sustained during our flight while still in the vicinity of our cave shelter. My comrade was wounded in the chest, and I in the waist. Our wounds had festered and were maggotty.

Soon it was time to continue our trek. The area we crossed was infested with Americans. We crawled on all fours most of the time to avoid them. In the process, we completely crushed and spoiled the precious potatoes in our pockets. The loss was so serious and the way it happened so ludicrous that we laughed and cried in turn.

At a well in the village of Miyagi, near Kiyan, we drank our fill and sat down to discuss our situation. My comrade, a new conscript only twenty-two years old, finally decided to go on with a Japanese soldier who happened by. I went my own way alone. But before long I met two soldiers, one from my own village; and the three of us agreed to continue together. The Japanese army under Lieutenant General Ushijima had abandoned Shuri and, under heavy American attack, was moving southward to establish new defensive lines. We joined them.

At Mabuni, on the southern coast, we heard Americans appealing to us to surrender and promising not to hurt us if we came out unarmed. Many of the Japanese hiding in caves along the coast doubted the American promises. Others climbed the hills and started to surrender only to be shot by their own comrades in the Japanese army. Still others, driven to the water's edge, chose suicide instead of surrender. Toward the end of June, we heard that General Ushijima himself had committed ritual suicide.

We then decided that the time had come to give ourselves up. Moving along a hill, we suddenly encountered an American who was not looking our way. We had our hands up in surrender; but turning around suddenly, he was so shocked to see us there that he threw his own hands skyward. I could not help laughing. Realizing his mistake at once, he quickly aimed his rifle at us. We were soon joined by other Americans, who searched us and took us to a prisoner camp at Yaka, where there were already many Japanese soldiers.

Five or six days later we were put on an American ship bound for Hawaii. We stopped for a while off Tinian when intelligence reports claimed that Japanese submarines were frequenting the area. But then we continued on our way.

We spent Christmas and New Year in a prisoner-of-war camp in Hawaii, where we were treated humanely for over a year. We had plenty of food — roast turkey on holidays — and cigarettes. In the prison hospital, doctors examined and treated my wound, which soon healed.

We had always been taught that Americans are brutes and savages; but in the prison camp, I learned different. Frankly, the kindness with which they treated me led me to think them nobler than the Japanese.

Japanese-Americans in Hawaii gave us radios over which we learned of Japan's defeat and of the numbers of survivors in various parts of Okinawa. We were greatly discouraged and disheartened to hear the emperor's surrender message.

When I returned to my home after a year's absence, I was overjoyed to find my wife in good health and my small son growing fast. Sometimes I still talk in my sleep about the camp in Hawaii.

Miraculous To Have Survived
Mitsuko Matayoshi

MY HUSBAND WAS A SOLDIER, but he had been reported missing. When word came that American forces had landed on Okinawa, my mother, her thirteen-year-old brother, my one-year-old child, and myself took refuge with three hundred people in a mammoth cave in Shuri. Later, Japanese army forces made us leave; they wanted the shelter for themselves. We went to Aragusuku, on the southern coast of the island. It was late at night when we arrived and found shelter in an old burial mound. After a few days, my mother's brother went out to draw water and did not return for a long time. I found him dead near the well,

45

probably hit by a shell. I covered his face with a basket that I found on the ground and returned to tell my mother of his death.

Soon enemy planes forced us from our shelter. We started out for a place called Yoza and on the way encountered a wounded soldier who had crawled on hands and knees all the way from a hill in Shuri. He had survived by sucking sugar cane and eating spoiled potatoes others had abandoned by the road. Though he had bandaged them with rags torn from his clothing, his wounds were infested with maggots. When I gave him some food, he was deeply grateful and expressed his feelings over and over.

Then the going became very rough for us. Heavy rains had converted the roads into swamps. With my baby strapped to my back, I struggled along. None of the many soldiers and refugees offered to help when, as often happened, I fell into the mud. The mire soon sucked the shoes from my feet, and I was forced to trudge along barefoot. The stones cut and bruised my feet. But the enemy troops had broken through Japanese lines and were on the way toward us. We had to go on.

In Yoza, we spent about ten days in a shelter, where we nearly starved. My breasts had dried up, and my infant was half dead from malnutrition. As enemy troops approached, the Japanese soldiers who shared the shelter with us started to leave. They agreed to take us with them only if I left my infant behind. I refused, and they left us. Then the sounds of enemy gunfire close at hand terrified me so that, putting some water and dried bread by his side, I abandoned the child and fled in pursuit of the Japanese soldiers. I was too frightened to have any sense of guilt.

Along our desperate way, we heard that a flash flood had swept through a shelter in the northeast, connected to the Gyo-kusendo Caverns. The refugees in the shelter had been drowned. Their bodies were floating at the mouth of a nearby river. We had been headed for that very shelter.

Mother and I then hurried back to Yoza, where we dashed in-to a shelter dug in the ground beside a house. Once again, we shared the place with Japanese soldiers. This time, the men

46

quietly sang military songs to boost the general morale, until a
shell exploded nearby, caving the roof in and burying alive all the
people in the inner part of the shelter. I saw their hands thrust up
from the earth when I revived from the faint into which I had
been thrown by the blast. My mother too had escaped. The two
of us hurried into another shelter not far away.

In the evening, as I went to draw water, I saw Japanese soldiers
firing machine guns at an American reconnaissance plane. It flew
away, to be followed by other American planes that strafed the
area, killing three of the Japanese soldiers. I was so fightened that
I forgot all about drawing water.

Shortly after I returned to the shelter, one of the soldiers ripped
off all his clothes and rushed naked out into the field, shouting,
"The war's over!" At about that moment, a mortar shell fell
through the roof, igniting the straw on the floor of the shelter. As
mother and I covered our heads with pieces of blanket and rushed
out, we saw the mad, naked soldier lying on the ground, charred
like a roasted goat.

Finding no bomb shelters nearby, we hurried into a thatched
farmhouse, where there were some more Japanese soldiers, many
of them injured. As we were about to settle down there, a bomb
fell through the roof. Everything went black. As I passed out, I
had the notion that at last death had come. Some time later, I revived to find my mother spared and myself relatively unharmed.
The flesh of blasted soldiers was clinging to walls and hanging
from trees in the yard.

Not knowing where we were going, we dashed through the
night, luridly lighted by the flares of the Americans and made
ghoulish by the shadows of Japanese soldiers carrying mines and
charging at enemy gun positions. I had to use a cane to hobble as
best I could on the toes of my cut, blistered, and swollen feet.
Soldiers carried wounded officers on boards, but ignored the
pleas for help of the common soldiers lying in pain on the ground.
As we darted here and there on our way to the southwestern end
of the island, I suddenly stepped on something that felt like an in-

flated inner tube. It was the bloated corpse of one of the many dead people we saw.

Finding a cave in a cliff, we went in and waited. Before long, Americans called over loudspeakers, asking us to come out and promising to treat us well. But their tanks frightened us so much that we ran toward the sea. The men who could swim jumped into the water and headed for a distant shore. But my mother and I joined a group of about twenty people resigned to wait for capture.

Among our group was a former prison guard with his wife and six children. His fourteen-year-old daughter had been wounded in the thigh by a shell. Her flesh was already maggot-ridden. The father wanted to take all the other children to the safety of an internment camp first and then to return for her. She could not walk on her own. She screamed and pleaded not to be left behind, but her father would not heed her. The elderly grandmother stayed behind to watch after the girl, who, seeing her family abandon her, began cursing and swearing in foul language that she would never forgive her father. The old woman seated by her side was deaf and could not hear her oaths.

Before moving toward the frightening group of black and white Americans not far away, my mother and I covered our faces with dirt and soot to make ourselves as unattractive as possible. There was no knowing what they would do. As we stepped into the blinding sun from the grove where we had been hiding, Japanese soldiers who did not intend to give themselves up whispered for us to be on our guard.

The Americans lined us up and searched us before taking us to a prisoner-of-war camp at Gushikami. On the truck, American soldiers offered us cigarettes and candy. We were so afraid that they might be poisoned that we would not accept them even when the Americans themselves ate in an attempt to prove that the food was safe. At the camp I was relieved to see many familiar people. On the morning after our arrival I asked the former prison guard what had happened to his abandoned daughter.

48

He said the Americans would not let him return because the place was too dangerous. He could only hope that she had been found and taken to an internment camp.

After a while we were shipped to an internment camp at Yambaru, where many people were dying of malaria and malnutrition. Perhaps because of the nagging, anguishing memory of my lost child, I went to work in the camp orphanage. The children I cared for not infrequently died of sickness, but there were always more orphans to take their places. One small girl pleaded with me to sleep with her. In the night I awakened to find her body stiff and cold next to mine. The following day she was laid in a small pit dug by the sanitation team. Her six-year-old brother sprinkled a handful of soil on her before the team covered her forever.

Owing to our horrible experiences and to malnutrition, most of us women working in the orphanage had stopped menstruating. Later, thanks to the food the Americans gave us, we regained our health; and our bodies began to function normally again. It is miraculous that I survived at all.

A Life Wrecked
Teru Matsue

AS THE FIGHTING in World War II neared Okinawa, I moved to Nago to be with my husband, who was in charge of a land-development project and had offices in a former hospital there. More than 1,000 workers were involved in the project; and my husband and his staff managed the shipments of rice, bean paste, soy sauce, and other staples brought to Nago from Naha by truck and horse cart.

I was pregnant at the time; and on August 10, 1944, I gave

49

birth to our elder son. To celebrate the baby's first month, I returned to Matsuda, where we had lived formerly, to visit my family. One day my elder sister and I prepared some special food for kind friends in Nago and had it sent there by horse cart.

When I awakened the following morning I decided to make some tea. Drawing water from the well, I returned to the house and put the kettle on. For some reason I squatted, and this saved my life. At that very second, the kettle was propelled from the top of the stove by a burst of machine-gun fire. Then I heard gunfire from Nago Bay. Seizing my baby and hastily putting on one of the air-raid hoods we all had at the time, I dashed from the house and jumped into the open sewer of a nearby school. Other people were there, as well. One woman, noticing that I had forgotten to bring diapers for the baby, chastised me as a disgrace to Japanese womanhood. But safety was all that I could think of.

After a while, the people in the sewer decided to flee into the mountains. I had to go with them. But unaccustomed to climbing and still weak from childbirth, I was soon exhausted. Still, somehow I managed to drag myself to the air-raid shelter in the mountains. Once again, the women in the party scolded me, this time because the baby cried continuously. But there was nothing I could do. He was hungry, and my breasts had dried up.

Two days later, when the all-clear sounded, the news that the island of Ieshima had been heavily attacked brought grief and tears to many mothers among us: their children, sixth-grade primary school pupils, had been sent to Ieshima to dig air-raid shelters.

Soon the defense corps came and ordered us to leave the mountain. I rose to go but could barely walk. I had been unable to bring food with me and was dizzy from two days of hunger. Fortunately, one of the people in our shelter kindly gave me a rice ball, which dulled the hunger pangs and gave me strength to begin the trip. Just then, however, one of the workers from my husband's project arrived with a horse cart and gave me a ride. On reaching Nago, I found the office in which we had been living riddled with holes from machine-gun fire. If I had been there when the fighting started, I would certainly have been killed.

My husband was nowhere to be seen, and I decided to return to Matsuda as quickly as possible. Strapping my baby to my back, I set out to walk, though every minute I was terrified of possible attacks from the air. Once again, I was fortunate enough to meet someone I knew—this time a cousin—with a horse cart. He drove me all the way to Matsuda.

On October 10, 1944, we experienced our second major air raid. Our house was severely damaged by machine-gun fire this time. The two shelters we had dug near the house were filled with foodstuffs; we took refuge in the much safer caves. Many people who had fled from Nago were in the caves with us. I cooked food for them.

When a temporary all-clear sounded, I took one of our workers with me to Nago in order to salvage food supplies we had left in the office and storerooms. But we were too late. The Japanese military had already occupied our buildings and refused to allow us to remove any of our food.

When the final air raid on Okinawa came, I was living in a cave with my child, an uncle, and other refugees. With the aid of searchlights, the Americans located our village and intensified their attacks. The able-bodied gradually left the cave to dig air-raid shelters in the mountains. Learning that my husband, too, was there and that he was unable to join us, I took my child to one of the mountain shelters.

Though the shelling and bombardments grew more furious, at night I would leave the shelter and climb up and down the mountains in search of my husband. The Americans, who no longer fired flares in the mountains, left the area at about seven in the evening. This made it easier for us to move about. In my wanderings, I encountered many unexpected things. Once I came upon American soldiers clearing roads and repairing bridges that Japanese troops had damaged. Late one night, I even ran into my elder brother. Finally, after three days of searching, I found my husband. Because the Americans had entered our village, I had feared I might never see him again. We wept with joy at our reunion.

American military aircraft began dropping leaflets informing us that the United States forces were not at war with the ordinary people. They told us to try to remain calm and to care for ourselves. The leaflets warned not to go to the beaches and to stay in the mountains. Finally, they admonished, "You cannot win fighting with bamboo spears against shells. If you love your homes, do not resist. Remain in the mountains. The Americans will soon land and bring you good food. Wait a little longer."

Although we knew that it was true that bamboo spears were useless against artillery, we did not trust the leaflets and refused to listen to any kind of advice until we ultimately learned of Japan's defeat.

Shortly before the end of the war, when the Americans had firm control of the island, word got out that their military police were arresting people from the main Japanese islands. My husband was one such person. He found it necessary to remain in the house at night and to hide in the mountains during the day. The Okinawans are somewhat darker in complexion than the Japanese, from the north. Men like my husband, with paler skin, tried to disguise themselves by smearing ashes on their faces, allowing their beards to grow, and wearing ragged clothes.

In the year that I had been forced to spend hiding and fleeing, I had ruined my eyesight and developed a wracking cough that made my relatives fear that I might not have long to live. Americans patrolling the area noticed that I was too ill to leave the house and soon brought a team of medical workers to examine me. They spoke no Japanese, and I understood no English. But they had provided themselves with a paper on which pertinent questions—"Where does it hurt?"—were written in Japanese characters. My poor eyesight forced me to strain to see each word; nonetheless, I answered their questions somehow. The medical team wrote down what I said and promised to return to take me to their hospital.

When the war was over, the American military provided tents for people whose houses had been destroyed and issued to every-one a variety of canned foods. We were able to remain in our own house.

At about nine o'clock one night, a group of twenty or thirty Japanese soldiers from the Miyazaki Unit came to us looking for food. Some of them were covered with lice. Feeling sorry for them, my husband gave them a bag of rice he had hidden behind the ceiling boards. He also gave them bean paste, sugar, and soy sauce. Some of the rice in our house had been drenched in rain and had fermented, producing a kind of homemade sakè. The soldiers were delighted to have some of the alcoholic drink and to eat the rice that we cooked for them.

One moonlight night a month later, we heard a voice calling softly from outside, "Matsue-san, I'm from the Miyazaki Unit. I want to thank you for helping us not long ago. Please come out-side."

My husband leaped from bed and went outdoors. As soon as he stepped through the door, several armed Japanese soldiers sur-rounded him and accused him of receiving things—including a pistol—from the Americans. My husband explained that he had hidden in the mountains by day and, as of yet, had not come face to face with an American. The Japanese would not believe him and ordered the house searched. My small child, mistaking one of the soldiers for his father, grabbed the man by the leg. The soldier kicked the boy brutally. I screamed frantically, "Why are you doing this? My husband is an honest man. Americans come here to see me because I am sick. But my husband never sees them or has anything to do with them. Don't harm him. Kill me instead. I'm only a sick woman."

In reply, the soldier slapped me in the face and called me a stupid fool. I fell to the floor.

53

Because they had watched what my husband did when he gave them food before, these men knew where our supplies were. They took everything they could find and left. Many of the people in our village had cooked rice and sweet potatoes and had carried them to mountain hideaways to feed just such men as these. This was the thanks they showed civilians for their kindness.

In general, the Americans did not mistreat the civilians, though they brooked no resistance, even if it was the result of a misunderstanding. People who did not come when called by the Americans were liable for beatings. One of our workers, a man who had planted sweet potatoes before the end of the war because he anticipated a food shortage, was shot when he ran from an American. He misunderstood the American's order to go to a prison camp to work in its fields.

As they had promised, the American medical team came for me when they had a vacant bed in their hospital, which had been set up in the Ginoza primary school. In other beds around me, many people lay suffering and dying. In the wounds of some of them maggots crawled. One death followed another in rapid succession, and I was afraid. I wanted to go home. One day, during the lunch hour, I managed to escape.

When I reached our house, I found it filled with refugees who had left the mountains in response to calls from the Americans and were occupying any vacant buildings they came upon. They slept on the floors and cooked and ate canned foods given them by American soldiers.

Food was short, and the Americans decided to ease the strain of the demand by repatriating all people from the main islands. My husband's name was on the list of those to go. At the time, I was pregnant with our second son and was suffering so badly from a high fever that I could not travel. My husband said that he would prefer to remain with me until I was well, but this was not allowed. He was sent back. I later learned that he was detained for two months in a concentration camp before being allowed to

54

return to his home in Kumamoto, on the island of Kyushu. While in the camp, he sent me a letter by way of a friend. He encouraged me by saying, "I will check the situation at home. If everything is all right, I will come for you. If you want to remain in Okinawa, I will return and stay with you. Until we meet again, be courageous and bring up our son and the new baby to be good, righteous citizens. Take the very best care of yourself."

In January, 1947, six months after my husband's repatriation, our second son was born. I received one more letter from my husband. He had found Kumamoto destroyed as the result of incendiary bombings. He was unable to locate his mother but intended to continue looking for her. I never heard from him again. He must have died while searching for his mother.

At the time of his last letter, our elder boy was three years old; and our younger, a newborn infant. Some of the people in our neighborhood went to work for the Americans, but I had no desire to do so. I planted sweet potatoes and gathered and sold firewood for a living. When my elder boy was seven, I returned to my native town on the island of Kume. My father told me that my older sister had been at Mabuni, on Okinawa, during the war and that nothing was known of her fate. While we were making plans to try to find her, he suddenly died. I remained in Kume until my elder son was in the second year of primary school; then I returned to Okinawa, to the city of Naha. Official documents showed that we had been repatriated to the main islands and that our records had been removed from the local files. Although this is merely one instance of postwar confusion, for my children it meant the tragedy of having no official name. I was told that I could have the matter cleared up in court, but I lacked the money to undertake legal action. Somehow I managed to get the children through primary and middle schools, but senior high schools would not accept them without an official family register. Finally, though I hated the idea of abandoning their true names, I had the children registered in the name of my own elder brother. To this day, my children are not able to use the name of their own father.

Demoralized Military

Sumi Tonouchi

IN 1945, THE MILITARY PREPARATIONS made because word
had arrived to the effect that war would come to Okinawa
horrified me and made me tremble. I could not believe that my
home island was to become a battlefield. In April, the Americans
landed. Fighting grew so fierce that all of us in the village of
Fukuchi were forced to flee for shelter. Over one hundred of us
crowded into a natural cave while our village became the scene of
fierce land attacks and air raids. American ships were lined up offshore to the south. In the daytime, fearful and miserable, we huddled back to back, knees drawn up, in the cramped cave. At
night we risked our lives by going out in search of food in spite of
the American flares that illuminated the entire area.

One day, the Japanese military ordered the young men and
women in our group to help transport ammunition to a dugout in a
nearby village where soldiers were holding out. Though terrified,
I helped with the work. Each time I stepped out of the cave, I was
filled with the fear of imminent death.

As the Americans advanced, the Japanese troops were pushed
farther and farther south. Japanese soldiers began frantically seeking shelter. They spotted our cave and ordered us out. Anyone
who hesitated or moved too slowly was beaten. With rage, I
watched a Japanese soldier strike an old man with a staff.

I was with my mother, my elder sister, and her child. We did
not know where to go. We fled, hand in hand for extra safety,
until we encountered a squad of Japanese mountain troops near a
village called Yamashiro. For some time we helped these men,
but soon they went to the front. Left alone again, the four of us
returned to Fukuchi, where we joined sixteen other villagers in a
dugout. But we were not allowed even this shelter for long. Soon
Japanese soldiers came and forced us to give our dugout to them.

56

I was appalled that we should be treated in this coldblooded way even though we had been devoted to the interests of the Japanese army.

We left our dugout at about daybreak and tried to escape in a rain of shells from the American ships in the offing. One shell that struck immediately in front of me knocked me to the ground. It killed one of my relatives who had been walking just ahead. After the initial shock, discovering that I was unwounded, I quickly ran away.

Later our group took shelter in a house near our ancestral cemetery. We were there for about twenty hours when an old man left the building to smoke. Americans on ships offshore spotted the glow of his cigarette and opened a blistering cannonade. One shell hit the roof of the house we were in, forcing us once again to abandon our wretched shelter.

By this time, the situation was so grave that the Japanese army was trapped in a southern corner of the island. We too moved southward, to a place called Cape Kiyan; but we found no cover there except the bushes and rocks and received no assistance from the Japanese troops, who forced us, at gunpoint, to hand over to them the meager rations of rice we had managed to bring with us.

Finally, trapped between American assaults from sea and land, we were captured on June 25, 1945, and transported by truck through the devastated, black, and treeless land to the Kin Concentration Camp. After four months in the camp, I was allowed to return to Itoman, where I found only the misery of the aftermath of war.

Women went foraging for food in terror of being raped by American soldiers who kept a keen eye out and never missed the chance to make such sexual attacks. I actually witnessed a friend being forced to yield to the lust of an American soldier.

To this day, I curse the brutality of the demoralized Japanese and American military; the miseries of defeat; and the horrors of war, which robbed our family of my eldest brother and profoundly grieved my mother, who loved him deeply.

Last Days of the Lily Corps

Sachiko Ishikawa

IN 1945, WHEN IT WAS FEARED that the American forces were about to make a landing on Okinawa, I was a second-year student in the Okinawa Prefectural Normal School. Every afternoon, after the regular classes, medical officers and non-commissioned officers of the medical corps conducted training in the school auditorium for all students above the second year in the normal school and all students in the third and fourth years of the Okinawa Prefectural First Higher School for Girls. Many of us were to join the Lily Corps, a group of young girls serving military medical units in the final days of the battle of Okinawa.

After the air raid that occurred on March 23 of that year, when it was clear that the American landing was imminent, the Haebaru Primary School was converted into a military hospital. Trench shelters dug around the school building were to accommodate hospitalized patients when the Americans landed. March 25 was to have been our graduation day, but the air raid changed everything, for the group of young girls with whom I had been training was assigned at once to the hospital in the Haebaru school. We had become members of the Lily Corps and of the armed forces.

Because our school dormitory had already been partially damaged in an air raid on the city of Naha on January 27, we had been forced to salvage what we could and build crude huts for ourselves among the hospital shelters at Haebaru. Our huts had two doors and no windows. After the air raid of March 23, we transported everything, pots and pans, rice, and other essentials, to the huts, where we continued to sleep until the Americans finally landed. We spent the days in the hospital shelters.

Artillery bombardment intensified as the days passed. Our

58

graduation, a simple candlelight ceremony held for students dressed in military uniforms, took place on the night of March 29. Since going home was now out of the question, we stayed on to serve. The situation got steadily worse. We were forced to spend most of our time in the shelters. I believe it was on April 1 that the American troops landed on Okinawa.

First-year students looked after the wounded in the shelters, while the rest of us helped in the hospital kitchen. One day we were given bamboo spears and told to fight the enemy with them because we had no other weapons. Actually we never used the spears.

As the Americans landed, the number of Japanese wounded increased so much that the first-year students were no longer able to care for them unaided. The rest of us were called on and were officially assigned as field nurses in the first, second, and third surgical departments. Since we were only from sixteen to nineteen years old, we were shy about waiting on wounded men and carrying bedpans for the ones who were unable to get up. But this was no time for shyness; we all had our work to do.

About thirty patients occupied the double bunks in each shelter. It was terrible there. The wounded cried for relief from pain and for changes of bandages. When they pleaded aloud for water, we wanted to stop their crying by giving it to them but knew we could not as it would only cause bleeding.

The pressure on us was great. The men in the shelters often clutched at us for help as we passed. We worked in two shifts: night and day. Usually we were in pairs, but sometimes one girl was forced to carry the burden alone when her partner collapsed from lack of sleep or exhaustion.

It became our task to remove the bodies of men who had died in treatment. It was too narrow in the shelters to use stretchers. One of us would have to hold the head and the other the feet. We had to drag out bodies that were too large and heavy for us to carry. When we had managed to get the corpses outside, we transferred them to stretchers so that we could carry them to the burial trenches dug by the medics. It still gives me chills of horror to think of those experiences.

Though less grisly, other tasks were ardous and dangerous. We had to carry supplies in large bundles from the storehouses to the trenches. In doing this, we had to be careful to conceal ourselves from the eyes of the enemy. But the most frightening work was the long trek we had to make through enemy fire to reach the field kitchen where food was prepared for the entire hospital. As we carried the food back through rains of bullets, I sometimes hoped I would be slightly injured so that I could stay in the shelters and not have to make these terrifying food runs. My emotions were always mixed. I was afraid of dying and hoped to live to see the day of victory that our militaristic indoctrination had taught us was sure to come. It never occurred to me that we might lose the war.

By the end of May the proximity of the Americans — only five hundred meters away — created such grave danger that it became necessary to move the hospital and to separate the various departments in the move. Previously all three surgical departments had been together on the mountainside south of Haebaru Primary School. Now they were to be scattered to distances of as much as two kilometers apart. The third department was to be located at the place where the Lily Corps Monument stands today. I was with the second surgical department.

It was raining hard on the night the move began. The Americans were immediately in front of us as we scrambled out of the shelters and headed over the mountain. Bullets whizzed around us as we moved to unknown destinations. It is unusual to relocate army hospitals, but we were in such a dangerous position at the front that there was nothing else to do.

Ambulatory patients were given army rations — two bags of hard, flavorless biscuits and two cans of scallops. We received the same provisions. But since we were required to carry gauze bandages, medicines, and dried bonito, we had to limit our clothes to the minimum.

It was impossible to carry the bedridden; they were left behind. In those days we were taught that it was more honorable to die than to become a prisoner of the enemy. The patients remaining in the shelters were given milk containing potassium cyanide. All those who drank it were listed as killed in action.

The move was costly in terms of life. The wounded straggled along in weariness and pain. Those who could not walk dragged themselves by means of the strength of their arms and buttocks in the hope of surviving. Infections and disease caused many to drop by the wayside. When we reached the Yoza spring, the former watering place of the village of Takamine, we learned that some of our fellow students, who had left earlier, had been killed in a direct bomb strike. But we were in no condition to bury them. Two members of our own party of students died. One was killed by machine-gun fire that shot off one of her legs. The other was buried alive in a bomb explosion; she was dead when we dug her out.

Though we were separated from others of our group, we struggled on, asking for directions whenever possible. Ultimately, we arrived at a place called Itosu (present-day Itoman), where most of us in the second surgical department went first to the house of a younger schoolmate. Shelters in Itosu had been dug by a mountain-troop unit that had later moved to the front, leaving the shelters for us to occupy. For a while we lived in relative peace. Though air raids continued, there was no gunfire close at hand.

But this peace did not last long. The enemy continued to advance along Okinawa, which is a narrow island. Air raids forced us to stay in the shelters in the day; but at night, when raids were infrequent, we would visit nearby homes. One night, however, the intensity of the raids increased. Intuition gained from experience told me that we were likely to come under naval bombardment soon. The next day, we remained in the shelter; but at night some of the nurses and medics went to surrounding private homes as usual. American naval bombardment hit those houses, killing many and injuring many more. The cries of the wounded were horrible.

On some days I felt certain that my own death was imminent. To our shock, the enemy came as far as the shelter where we were working. Once a grenade was thrown in through a hole, and outside I heard people talking in some language that was not Japanese. We had been told that it would be another week before the enemy reached us.

Suddenly, in the afternoon of June 19, 1945, the Americans occupied the hill commanding Itosu. We were sitting in the hot shelter — there was only one opening — discussing the situation. We still thought we had time before the enemy would arrive. Then, in a flash, we were fired on. The shelter was so small that everyone in second surgical could not get inside at one time. Someone was always forced to sit just under the cover at the door. On this day Michiko Miyagi, who was under the entrance cover, was hit in both knees. Yaeko Wauke was slightly wounded in the buttocks, and one patient was killed.

Confused by the suddenness of the attack, we all sat terrified, packed into the sweltering shelter. One of the medics murmured to himself, "The enemy has come." The only soldiers in the stifling place were a few medics armed with nothing but some grenades. There was nothing that we could do to drive the Americans away. We had heard that when they commanded a position like the one they held at Itosu the Americans usually destroyed whatever shelters they found. Feeling that our fate was sealed and that survival was impossible, doctors Yonamine and Uchida, who were in charge of our department, discussed future action with the students. We all agreed that if death was upon us we would stay together. Our decision to die in a group was reported at once to the captain who was acting as chief surgeon.

In the long silence that prevailed in the shelter, I thought of the

62

happy things that had happened to me when I was four or five and of my days at the normal school. My short life of less than twenty years was about to end; I had so many things I wanted to remember. My parents were both dead. I forced myself to believe that in dying I would join them.

In the breathless silence, I sweated and waited for the attack that I feared would come at any minute. But by nightfall there had been no attack.

Heat and thirst aggravated our suffering. Finally, the army surgeon began to urge us to leave the shelter. At first, we hesitated. Then, deciding that if we had to die it would be better at least to have a drink of water first, we went out, one by one. The army surgeon had preceded us and was observing the situation carefully. It took until about three o'clock in the morning for all of us to leave the shelter. Even after the decision to go was made, we hung back in fear of being shot. Then a junior school-mate of mine said, "I don't care anymore. If I'm going to die, I'm going to die; and that's that." She went out. No sound of firing was heard. We all began to think we would be able to make it and started leaving.

The scene outside the shelter was weird: silence and the eerie light of flare bombs. We had heard that Americans did not fire when they surround a place in this way for fear of shooting their own men.

Nearby was a spring toward which we all ran, only to be forced to hide fast when we discovered that the Americans were already there. When a flare bomb hit, we all fell to the ground and rose to run only when it became dark again.

The second surgical department, to which I belonged, disband-ed. We decided to try to make contact with the first and third surgical departments; but on our way to their location, some dis-tance from our shelter, we were forced to hide from an American patrol. We found shelter with a group of Japanese soldiers who allowed us to stay with them for a while when we explained our situation. Soon the soldiers said that they would have to move on.

We were wondering what to do next when we came in contact with the first surgical department. It was June 19. None of us cared much what happened, since we were resolved that death was all that awaited us. We still had not been able to quench our scorching thirst.

The Japanese soldiers had stopped resisting. They simply lacked materiel and ammunition. But the well-equipped Americans continued to press forward. For each shot fired by a Japanese, they would answer with a hundred. The bullets kicked up dust as, in their abundance, they hit the same spot over and over. Those of us who could use the military shelters were lucky. Civilians who lacked such refuge were often killed while attempting to hide behind trees.

On the morning of June 20, we left our shelter in hope of finding escape routes near Cape Kiyan. But the Americans were virtually on top of us. There was nowhere to go.

I had nothing to wear but the trousers and shirt I had worn when we left the second surgical department. Whenever it rained and I had to hang my clothes up to dry, I was left naked. Then I remembered the cloth and gauze I had been given for use if injured. Fortunately, I had a needle and some thread and a pair of scissors. Sitting under a tree, I made underclothes from the gauze and cloth.

Food was difficult to obtain. We all lay still, hiding, during the day and at night stole to nearby fields to dig up the string-thin potatoes that grew wild there. No one tended the land anymore, and whatever there was to eat was assumed to belong to the finder. For a while we built fires for cooking behind big rocks at night. Some of the civilians shared their salt and bean paste with us. With these meager materials, we were able to survive on cooked potatoes. But soon we were unable to build fires, and the potatoes ran out.

As the end of the battle of Okinawa approached, the Americans intensified their shelling. Scores of artillery and mortar shells

64

might be fired in one minute. They would envelop us with white smoke and the stench of powder from as far away as a kilometer. Whenever the Americans spotted a group of people, they opened fire. At first, this happened only in the day; but later the raids continued into the night.

There was almost no drinking water. Once I managed to get a bucketful from some local people, but I lost it all when an explosion occurred as I was trying to get back to our camping site. Many soldiers were killed in that explosion.

We were completely surrounded by American troops. All of us who had no way of escaping were grouped together. We ran out of food and were forced to chew sugar cane. When the Americans saw this, they tried to destroy our last food supply by burning the cane fields.

Nisei American soldiers addressing us over loudspeakers from the ships on the sea urged us to give ourselves up by walking to a sandy beach located about twelve hundred meters away. They warned that if we did not do as they ordered they would open fire. We did not surrender, and they did open fire.

As long as their shots fell on the other side of the rocks we were using for shelter, we were safe. But when the shells fell on our side, we were in grave danger. Many people died.

Then we came to the conclusion that our only hope of escape was to jump into the sea and swim for it. One night, I tried it but found the waves too strong and returned to shore. Among the soldiers with us were some strong swimmers who tried at the same time as I. But they either drowned or were shot. Their bloated, whitened bodies washed up on shore the next day.

During the day, the Americans kept watch over us from tanks. At night, they sent up flares. One soldier who had swum to us from Mabuni said that there too the people were trapped. It was useless to flee to such a place. We tried to reach Itosu but failed because the rocks cut our feet so badly that we could no longer walk. The soldiers told us not to hurry, since all we had to do was wait for our own troops to land. Even then, people in Okinawa firmly believed that reinforcements would come from mainland Japan.

We lived for one month on the beach with virtually no food. By the end of July, our group of more than a thousand had dwindled to about twenty people. Escape by sea was impossible. We tried to flee by land but failed. Wherever there were lights at night, there were Americans and we could not avoid them.

One of the medics who had worked with us at the hospital kitchen suggested that there might be some kind of food left at the third surgical shelter site. We went there, only to be greeted by a sight of incredible horror. All the girl students in the third surgical department had been killed in action. We did not know this until we got there and saw their bodies, burned beyond recognition, some of them already partly skeletonized. Later I learned that the students who had died huddled together had been killed by enemy flame throwers.

Not far from the site of the third surgical department was a deep pit used as a garbage dump by Americans camped nearby. It soon became our source of food. Because the Americans did not move about at night, we were able to scavenge for leftovers in the garbage pit. We hid in the third surgical department shelter in the day. At night, a soldier would climb down into the pit on a rope. We would drop him another rope, with which we would lift the scraps of food he found. Civilians in the vicinity too came to the pit when they learned it was a source of edibles. This is what kept us alive.

During the period while we were in the shelter, the Americans became suspicious and searched but did not detect us. At night the only light we had was a lamp filled with oil squeezed from pork fat. A piece of cloth was the wick. Since we had very few matches, we kept the lamp burning throughout the day to avoid having to light it often.

On August 15, I was running a fever. When I heard heavy shooting outside, I assumed that our troops had finally landed and were trying to force the Americans to retreat. I later learned that the firing was by the Americans to celebrate the unconditional surrender of Japan.

A soldier who had been captured while searching for food came back to announce the end of the war. But the lieutenant with us refused to believe that Japan would surrender. Finally, however, he agreed to go out under a white flag to find out what was happening. He told us that if he did not return we would know that the rumor of surrender was a lie. We were then to remain where we were and to try to stick it out to the end. If Japan had indeed surrendered, he would return to tell us.

When a day had gone by without his returning, we began to feel that the rumor was false. Then, with a confused look on his face, the lieutenant returned with the news: Japan had surrendered.

Tears trickled down my face. I was sad that we had lost; but I was relieved not to have to dodge bullets any more. Okinawa was no longer ours. I wanted to run away; still, I wanted to stay. The indoctrination we had received, to the effect that Japan must win, caused me great perplexity.

Nonetheless, there was no longer any reason to hide in the shelter. We called to people in other shelters to tell them to come out. One naval lieutenant commander at first flatly refused to be taken prisoner. But a week later he too emerged from the shelter.

Three trucks came and took us to an internment camp near Hyakuna. Even after I arrived there, I was confused. One week had passed since the surrender. There was no more Lily Corps. A camp school—a school without buildings or facilities of any kind—had been opened; and some of the former teachers, with the help of graduates like me, were holding classes out of doors. Education had resumed.

But it had been the kind of education that we received earlier that had caused great sacrifices. Militarism had been deeply planted in our minds. When we left school, one of our teachers had told us that we did not have to stay with the Lily Corps and the troops. We could have gone home to relative safety. We replied that if necessary we were prepared to die for our country. Even if Okinawa were to be destroyed, as Saipan had been, it would be all right as long as Japan won the war. The young girls who now lie buried at the Lily Corps Monument never doubted Japan's ultimate victory. For the sake of that victory they sacrificed their lives. As I think back on it now, I realize how thoroughly we had been indoctrinated in the militaristic way of thought. Having experienced the war associated with it, I am strongly opposed to militaristic education.

Schoolboys to the Front

Yasunobu Inamine

WHEN UNITED STATES troops landed on Okinawa, our group of students at the Number Three Middle School in the town of Nago was organized into four companies that together were called the Blood and Iron Royalist Unit. Two of these companies were ordered to cooperate with the Udo Unit, which was commanded by our teacher Mr. Taniguchi. The other two were assigned to the Tama Unit. I was in the former.

Before starting for the front, all of us went home to tell our mothers of our assignments and to give them cuttings of our hair and our fingernail clippings, neatly wrapped in white paper, to keep as charms until we returned.

All of us had received military training ever since the time we began our education. We ranged in age from thirteen to seventeen. On the appointed day, we went to our school, where only the fourth-year students received arms: old-fashioned 38-model rifles from the school armory. All of us were going to test on the battlefield the art of killing that we had been taught at school.

68

We proceeded to Izumi Primary School, in Motobu, where I met my father. He had been called to fight in the National Defense Corps. Telling him that I had been home to see mother and was now on my way to the front, I said goodbye and wished him luck.

At Mount Yaedake, where we were assigned, we fortified our position to the best of our abilities. The war had taken a disastrous turn for Japan. From dawn till sunset, United States aircraft bombed and strafed us. Not a single Japanese plane was to be seen in the sky. The air attacks increased daily, and soon the Motobu Peninsula was subjected to ceaseless bombardment by United States warships. Many people, both military and civilian, died as the result of wounds from fragments of exploding shells. Unable to act in the day because of United States control of the air, Japanese forces were compelled to resort to night raids.

Before long, American troops began to land on the island from all sides. At night their flares illuminated the entire sky. Mortar raids on our positions sometimes killed as many as forty or fifty people at a time. As we became more accustomed to the incessant firing, we learned to estimate whether the shell was headed our way. On several occasions, I escaped death only because shells landing nearby failed to explode. Often a pine tree offered shelter from strafing attacks that nearly proved fatal to me. Taking advantage of their materiel superiority, the United States forces concentrated fire from air, land, and sea as if they were determined to destroy the whole Motobu Peninsula.

Kamikaze pilots were attacking ships on the sea. On land, their counterparts were first- and second-year students who carried explosives in their arms, lay in ambush, and hurled themselves like living bombs at approaching American tanks.

The members of our Blood and Iron Royalist Unit, armed with no more than swords, were eager to participate even in night attacks if doing so would help defend the nation. It sometimes happened that boys staging such attacks were exposed to fire from Japanese, not enemy, troops. Sometimes the pleas of the boys to halt fire did not reach the ears of their countrymen in time.

69

WHAT GOOD DOES THIS DO?

On one occasion, when the group that I was with came upon forty or fifty American troops about a hundred meters ahead, we begged our teacher to allow us to open fire. At the time we were armed with rifles. He refused, and the enemy finally disappeared before we had a chance to act. I was puzzled by the teacher's action then. Now I think I understand it. He realized that Japan was losing and he did not want to sacrifice his students. We had only six bullets each. If we had opened fire, the well-equipped Americans would easily have wiped us out.

Soon United States troops occupied all of the Motobu Peninsula. In their mopping-up operations, they took refugees to concentration camps. Our unit was forced to abandon our position and to trek across Mount Yaedake in an attempt to reach the remainder of the Udo Unit, located, we believed, on Mount Tano. But when we reached the location, we found only a few members of a voluntary defense corps, composed of local young men, who told us of a fierce battle that had taken place the previous day.

At Mount Tano we faced a concentrated enemy attack that almost annihilated our unit. Of the four hundred people who had started the campaign, only seven, including our teacher Mr. Taniguchi, had survived. He had hoped to lead us through the central part of Okinawa to Shimajiri, but he became ill. Because he said that he could not remain idle in sickness while we continued fighting, we decided to separate from him until his health improved. From that day, we lived in the forest like animals. One day, disguised as civilians, we were captured and taken to a concentration camp for refugees at Haneji. There we learned that the war had already ended.

After the Horror, a Homecoming

Keiko Karimata

BECAUSE OF MY EMPLOYMENT in an important shipyard in Tsurumi, Yokohama, I was put on reserve status and not in the regular military for a number of years. But in 1944, as many of my fellow workers were drafted one after the other, I feared that my turn would come soon. On January 15, 1944, the summons arrived. I was worried because my wife, who was pregnant at the time, our three children, and my elderly mother would be left without a man to care for them. Fortunately, the ninety yen my company agreed to pay as part of the premium on my life insurance policy would enable them to manage. Before I left to enlist in the navy, I told my wife to remain in Yokohama instead of returning to Miyakojima island, where we were both born.

No matter how they suffered personally from fear and apprehension about the welfare of their loved ones, Japanese soldiers in those days were not supposed to reveal their feelings. We had to put up the kind of brave front that was considered worthy of the armed forces of the Japanese Empire. With the then traditional exhortation not to return alive, I left in feigned high spirits, accompanied to the station by friends and relatives, all of whom were waving small Japanese flags. On that day, I noticed planes in the sky and thought that they were Japanese. It turned out that they were American bombers about to conduct a raid on Tokyo and the surrounding area. At the time, I had a hunch that Japan was going to lose the war. After all, it had already become necessary to call up men, like me, in their late twenties.

On the first day of my enlistment in the marine corps at the naval base at Sasebo, we were given a special treat of glutinous rice cooked with red beans (a dish usually served in Japan on auspicious occasions). But to our feast our superior officer added the comment: "That's the last fine food you're going to get. Things are not going to be soft from now on; make up your minds to that."

After receiving my uniforms, I sent my old clothes home to my wife. We had just built our own house in Tsurumi, and she was grieved to receive the package. Weeping as she put the clothes away, she thought, "He's gone to war now and may never come home again."

Life was not easy for us in the barracks. The thin blankets we were issued did not keep us warm at night. Our superior officer carried a large "training" stick with which he frequently hit us "to instill the military spirit in you," he said. The barracks were patterned on a ship. The right side was called starboard, and left port. Our officer lectured in an intimidating voice and banged on the floor with his training stick. "You guys might have been babied at home," he was fond of saying, "but in this outfit, anybody who enlisted ahead of you is your superior; and you'd better do what he says. Get it?" I disagreed with much that this man said and did, but disobedience was out of the question. For me, life at Sasebo was agony.

After Sasebo, I went to Ch'inghae, in what is today the Republic of Korea. From there I was to have gone to the front lines in the South Pacific; but fierce American attacks there and the worsening of the Japanese situation postponed our departure, apparently indefinitely. We were sent first to the Oita Naval Air Corps Base in Oita, on the island of Kyushu. Then, after a brief tour building antiaircraft positions at Sasebo, I volunteered to be sent to Okinawa, where I hoped to see friends and perhaps make a trip to nearby Miyakojima island. On October 10, we left Sasebo by ship and sailed to Kagoshima, where we put in until October 20.

I had received a letter earlier telling me that my wife, too, was now in Kagoshima. Life had become impossible for her in Tsu-

72

rumi. Taking the children with her, she had come to Kagoshima to wait for one of the very few boats then carrying civilians to Okinawa. Her wait was so long that she found it too expensive to continue paying for rooms in inns and rented a dilapidated little house. The time to give birth to our fourth child was rapidly drawing near.

When our ship landed at Kagoshima, all men with relatives in the region were permitted to go ashore. I went at once in search of my family. At the inn from which my wife had written, I learned she was no longer there. By chance one day, I happened to notice two boys quarreling in a side lane. One of them reminded me of my eldest son; and indeed, when I asked his name, he replied, "Takeshi Karimata." He had changed so much that I did not recognize him at first. I told him to take me to his mother.

In the shabby, small house sat my wife with our newly born fourth child. From the look on her face I could judge how great an ordeal she had suffered in giving birth under such circumstances. But I tried to hide my feelings in order to cheer her up.

Our large convoy—twenty-four transport ships sailing three abreast—left Kagoshima on October 21. I was on board the Tomitsu-maru, the third of the three lead ships. As we approached the mouth of Kagoshima Bay, one of the many American submarines infesting the waters fired torpedoes, missed the first two ships, but hit the Tomitsu-maru in the stern. After a tremendous explosion, the ship began to list and to fill with water rapidly. Pandemonium broke loose. Many of the men started to jump overboard; but brandishing a sword, the commanding officer threatened to cut down anyone who did not remain in his place.

After a short while, preparations for abandoning ship got under way. All of us marines were ordered to jump in heavily clothed—for some reason that I did not understand—and to swim as fast and far as possible. With a photograph of my family in my pocket, I leaped into the water. As we were swimming toward the several small, uninhabited islands in the vicinity, the Americans

73

torpedoed and sank a destroyer escort ship and the first transport. When the submarine had gone, a destroyer rounded us up and took us to Oshima. Covered with black crude oil cast up by the sinking ships and with weirdly glowing eyes, we must have been a strange sight.

On October 25, we were taken by ship from Oshima to Naha, Okinawa. We found the city in ruins owing to heavy air raids on October 10. Some of the sugar and rice warehouses were still burning.

I was to have been a ground-crew member for planes at Oroku Airfield, but the installation had been completely destroyed. There were no planes for me to service. Because of a total lack of barracks, we camped out at a place called Uebaru and worked from morning to night building gun emplacements and digging trenches.

On April 1, 1945, American forces, supported by the heaviest barrage of naval gunfire in the history of warfare, landed on the coast of Okinawa. In addition to the pounding guns of the ships swarming in the seas, the island was subjected to rains of bombs from carrier-based aircraft.

Japanese marines, under the command of Rear Admiral Minoru Ota were deployed largely in the southern part of the island. But there were small mobile bands for guerrilla and harassment tactics. I was a member of one of these bands. The Japanese command headquarters, under Lieutenant General Mitsuru Ushijima, were at Shuri, the center of the fiercest fighting.

Though the Americans were numerically superior and better equipped, Japanese troops resisted determinedly. Having gained a few hundred meters in the day's fighting, the Americans would retreat after dark out of fear of violent night reprisal attacks. With tremendous casualties on both sides, positions were taken, recaptured, and retaken. While these battles raged, the mobile forces, to which I belonged, staged nighttime guerrilla warfare. I was armed with a machine gun taken from a destroyed fighter plane.

74

Multichambered and of high-performance capability, it enabled me to fire a thousand rounds of ammunition without stopping.

Heavy rains turned roads into quagmires. Fields were strewn with swollen corpses.

On May 4, 1945, we gave up reconnaissance and harassment raids to participate in a massive, all-out counteroffensive that the imperial army mounted to try to turn the tide in the long battle of attrition conducted by the Americans.

At about sunrise that day, my small group was near the mouth of a cave where villagers and, according to rumor, the prefectural governor were in hiding. Suddenly a third-class petty officer was hit in the abdomen by a bullet. Realizing the gravity of his wound, he moaned in a low voice, "Hand grenade, hand grenade." He intended to commit suicide. But since we were in a place where explosives might injure people in the cave, we gave him potassium cyanide. By that time most of us carried either hand grenades or poison for just such purposes.

In our sector, the Japanese forces made no headway throughout the day. In fact, we lost ground. At night the Americans sent up flares, making everything as bright as day. Hungry and thirsty, we crawled along the road until we came to a stream. The flares were gone by this time. All was dark. We could not tell whether the water in the stream was clear or crimson with the blood of dead soldiers. But we drank it anyway.

We were isolated and had no way of finding out how the fighting was going. Apparently, we had little time left to live. It seemed better to try to go back to Oroku Airfield and to die among Japanese than to be killed among the Americans. In our crawl across the fields toward Oroku, we met some Japanese soldiers who told us that the army general offensive had failed and that the marine units taking part in it had disintegrated. They advised us to escape with them to the south of the island. We agreed.

At a deserted house on a hill near the village called Yone, we

75

decided to rest. After we wrung out our rain-drenched clothes and ate some small tomatoes that we found, we all felt tired and fell asleep.

It was already morning when we were awakened by a loud rumbling noise. We looked quickly in the direction of Oroku Airfield, thinking that the sound might be coming from there. To our bewilderment and terror we saw rank after rank of American tanks and American soldiers coming over the hill. As fast as we could, we ran away and continued southward along the coast. At a breakwater along the way, we found a Japanese soldier whose side had been ripped open by bullet fire. With blank, pleading eyes, he looked at us. But there was nothing we could do. Sorrowfully, we left the bleeding man and went our way.

Countless American ships fired from the distance whenever they spotted a human figure. Our journey was dangerous and hard, but finally we reached the river at Itoman. Because the bridge had been blown out, we had to swim. A strong swimmer, I made it across with a heavy machine gun on my back.

We were refused when we asked some of the hundreds of refugees in abandoned houses and under trees to be allowed to join them. Military personnel would only invite gunfire from American warships. We had to seek shelter elsewhere. But we filled our canteens from a nearby well before leaving.

Shortly afterward, the American naval bombardment intensified, and strafing attacks from the air became more violent. The refugees now fled to the hills; and I joined them, after camouflaging my machine gun with leaves and branches. By that time, mental and physical exhaustion had annihilated fear. I cared little whether I was hit or not.

Enemy naval fire had not reached the village of Ishiki, where I decided to rest at about noon. While I sat under a hedge, leaflets fell fluttering to the ground. I read one of them: "It is useless for Japanese soldiers to resist further. . . . Surrender immediately. . . . Both soldiers and civilians will be treated humanely if they give themselves up, abandon their weapons, and come out with their hands held over their heads." I dismissed all this as false-hood and deception.

In the evening, at a well where I went for water, I met one of the officers from my unit. He congratulated me on surviving and told me to come with him to our commander, who told me that though marine units had retreated from the southern central sector we had been ordered to defend Japanese positions on the southern tip of the island to the death.

A small group, including another Okinawan and me, was ordered to reconnoiter the region between Cape Kiyan and the village of Yamagusuku. It began to rain as we moved through a region in which trench-mortar fire was furious. Since this kind of fire does not fall twice on the same spot, we were able to advance slowly by taking shelter in the shell craters. We walked over countless unidentifiable human bodies. Soon our clothes, already ragged and mud caked, were impregnated with the stench of death. There were so many corpses that it was difficult to walk.

At Kiyan, on the southernmost tip of Okinawa, a small boy, crying "Mother, Mother!," clung fiercely to me. My companions warned that I could not carry out my mission hampered with the child. Still, he would not let me go, even when I bribed him with bread. He only went on crying, as he had probably been doing for several terrifying hours. Finally, though it broke my heart, I left him with a piece of dry bread and a false promise to return.

The next morning, as we fled from the machine-gun fire of air-craft, we spied a great cloud of black flies hovering in the air. They were over the crater created by a monstrous 500-kilogram bomb that had fallen directly on a large group of refugees. Dis-membered bodies covered the ground. Pines were hung with flesh and bespattered with blood. Severed arms and legs hung from the trees. Nauseated, we fled in horror.

Continuing on our way, we stopped to pick cane in a sugar field. Suddenly someone called, "Hey, you marines. Give me some water." It was a soldier who had lost both arms. At first, I thought I had no water left, but he said he could hear sloshing in my canteen. I checked and found a small amount of water there. I gave it to him and peeled sugar cane for him to eat. But we had to go on. We left him telling him we had a mission to accomplish.

Learning at Cape Kiyan that the enemy had built antiaircraft positions, pillboxes, trenches, and machine-gun emplacements along the coast and that the Japanese were engaged in battle in the area, we returned to our unit to report. We were then instructed to reconnoiter Mabuni, east of Cape Kiyan, and to confirm there the presence of Lieutenant General Ushijima, commander of the Thirty-second Army.

Before leaving on this task, we snatched up some boiled potatoes that refugees had dug the night before. On the way to Mabuni, we descended a flight of stone steps leading to a well. We were thirsty. But at the mouth of the well we discovered a mound of corpses, probably people killed by the enemy as they came out of the woods in search of water.

Performing the wildest acrobatic leaps and jumps, we finally made it through heavy enemy fire and naval bombardment to Mabuni, where all we learned was that the Japanese troops were putting up only weak resistance against the Americans, who were steadily closing in.

Our report to this effect convinced our squadron leader that it was time to make the hazardous journey to Mabuni, where we could at least join the main body of the Japanese forces. No one in the group had weapons except the lieutenant, who had kept his sword. Resistance was already futile.

The rocky coast offered very little cover for our flight. The Americans were carrying out extensive patrols and mopping-up operations. In one rocky cliff, I happened to find a hole under a rock. Peeping in, I saw five or six civilians hiding in a natural cave. We joined them. The infant of one of the women continually cried. After a while, our lieutenant shouted, "If your baby doesn't shut up, the enemy will find us. You'll have to get out of here." The woman wept in fear of what might await her outside. But our high-strung lieutenant was unmoved. Losing his

78

temper, he pulled his sword from its sheath and roared, "What's more important: our lives or your baby? If you don't get out right now, I'll cut you down!" She left.

Shortly afterward, I went out to urinate. Hiding behind a rock, I watched American amphibious craft come into the inlet near our shelter and systematically seal the openings of all caves with flame throwers, probably entombing unknown numbers of people inside. A destroyer came into the inlet too. But they did not spot our cave because it was concealed by a pile of rocks.

Nonetheless, the cave was clearly no longer a safe place to hide. We decided to penetrate the American lines and flee northward to Kunigami, in the central part of the island.

On the following morning we left the cave and soon came to a windbreak forest. Deciding to rest for a while, we joined a group of Okinawan refugees and Japanese soldiers, most of whom were occupying themselves by picking lice from their bodies. One woman — said to be starving — was tossing on the ground in pain. After a while, she stopped moving.

During the rest period, I took out some medical scissors and trimmed my shaggy beard. A girl who noticed what I was doing asked me to cut her hair. As I did so, countless lice fell from her head.

Before long we left the forest and headed again for Kunigami. But along the way, our squadron leader stepped on a wire trap that set off a sudden burst of machine-gun fire. He was killed instantly. The rest of us fled.

Now the Americans, talking in loud voices, came searching for stragglers. They were indiscriminately scorching everything with flame throwers. Two of my comrades and two young Okinawan girls who had decided to flee to Kunigami with us hid in a depression overgrown with Japanese pampas grass. The fire spread toward us. The heat was horrible. But if we budged, the enemy would shoot us. We endured; and soon the Americans went away, giving us the chance to sneak across the blackened fields to a village where we covered our faces with soot as a kind of camouflage and searched the pockets of the dead for rice. We were nearly starving. In the daytime, no Japanese soldiers were around. But at night they came out with Okinawan refugees and, ghostlike, wandered in search of food and water.

We too hid in the day and foraged at night. Sometimes we ate canned foods thrown away by the Americans. One night, we stumbled on a cave, where, by a faint light, we saw two Okinawan boys, members of the Okinawan defense corps. They had managed to salvage some food, which they stored in their cave. Though they gave us some boiled rice, a treat we had not had in a long time, they did not welcome our staying with them and being a drain on their scanty stock. But they were happier to have us after some of our group found rice, soy sauce, and unrefined sugar in a cave formerly occupied by Japanese troops. For months we stayed in the cave with the boys. At night we went digging in positions abandoned by the Americans and usually were able to find cigarettes, gasoline, and canned food.

In October we heard a loudspeaker announcing: "The war ended August 15. Come out of your caves." But we thought it was an enemy trick. One night we saw a cigarette burning in the darkness. It was a member of a placation squad who said, "We came to you at night because you won't come out during the day. We are afraid to come too close to you. You seem to be armed." We were, in fact, carrying automatic rifles that we had picked up at some American positions. The placation squad went away to find more definite information about the war. Two days later, American soldiers captured us and took us to a prisoner-of-war camp at Kin. Civilians were interned at a camp in Ishikawa.

One American soldier asked me to trade my Japanese fountain pen and some coins for cigarettes. He said he wanted them as souvenirs. But in front of the camp, he stripped me naked for inspection, took my pen, and refused to give me the cigarettes he had promised.

In three days we were moved to another camp, where we built our own shabby quarters out of tents and barbed wire. Each morning, the Americans gave us skimpy canned food that was supposed to last the day. But we ate it all at once. It was hard to work on an empty stomach all day. But sometimes we coaxed American soldiers into giving us something extra at lunch.

Life got no better. There was no sign that we were going to be demobilized; and we were transferred to another camp, where, in all kinds of cold and rain, we were forced to dispose of expended shells and cartridges.

About twenty-five men lived in one tent. Once I thought of running away and went so far as to write a letter asking a village headman to shelter me if I broke out. He told me to be patient and to wait.

We scrounged a lot of things while we were working. Noticing that Americans took beer, food, and clothing from warehouses without permission, we started doing the same. But one day military police came and took away all of our loot. I later heard that these confiscated goods were distributed to civilian refugees by the Americans.

In desperation, some of the prisoners shamelessly stole grain alcohol from the prison dispensary and got drunk. But we had wholesome pastimes too. There were volleyball, boxing, and baseball. Professional actors among the prisoners staged occasional plays in which men took all the female roles.

Some of the Americans guarding us were kind and gave us cigarettes. Others were mischievous—even malicious—and did things like firing pistols at the timbers we were carrying or at our feet.

Without word from my wife since our chance meeting in Kagoshima, I grew melancholy and gloomy. But at last, in December, 1946, I was demobilized. At first I went to Nagoya, where Okinawan repatriates assembled. I found many of my relatives there; but more wonderful, I learned the good news that my wife and children had been sent to our native Miyakojima island. I followed them on the next available boat, and we had a very happy reunion.

CHAPTER TWO

Whether There's Kids

You got to bury a guy somewhere
Funny I thought as I looked at him
Blackened, with a pair of holes for eyes,
You bury a stiff and there he lies,
And Christ only knows where he come from
And whether there's kids somewhere or a dame,
We buried him like he came in this world,
A stiff, naked, without a name.

ALFRED HAYES
"The Death of the Craneman"

When man wages war families are sundered. Those who embark for foreign battlefields may never return. Those who remain at home may never know what happened to lost loved ones. Fathers, struck down in their green, seeking youth, can never watch their children grow to the age of responsibility. Fathers, slaughtered while their seed grows in the woman's womb, never so much as see their infants. Families remaining together on friendly soil suffer to watch each other endure the hardships that war creates. Warriors on each side cherish photographs and memories of their beloved. But when they slay an enemy on the bloody field, do they wonder "whether there's kids" somewhere for the other guy too?

Light He Never Saw
Fumie Masaki

IN JULY, 1945, I was in the final month of pregnancy. On the eleventh, as planes droned overhead, my husband rushed from our seal-engraving shop, shouting, "Air raid!" An incendiary bomb fell directly on his head. He was instantly wrapped in a sheet of bluish flame from the sticky, oily contents of the bomb. I could not put out the fire. All my desperate efforts were of no avail.

Neighbors carried him to a medical relief center in a nearby school. His hair was still sizzling and giving off a blue light. His skin peeled away in sheets, exposing his flesh. I could not even wipe his body. A nurse walked around with scissors, clipping the burning hair from the heads of the wounded. "Enemy planes might spot it and drop more bombs," she said.

I nursed my husband as best I could through the night, but he died early the following morning.

Two days later, my third son, who had been evacuated to the country, was playing with some of his friends in a playground. The children found an unexploded bomb and reported it to the air-raid wardens. One of them came to the playground and tossed the bomb to see whether it was still live. It went off, injuring many children and killing eight, among them my son.

I rushed to the place as soon as I heard of the explosion. My son was still alive. When he saw me, he asked, "Where is Dad? How is he?"

"He's at home today. He's not feeling well," I lied.

"I wish I could see him. And, Mother, I made a doll for the new baby. I left it with my teacher. Please go and get it from him."

My kindhearted, intelligent boy died in a few minutes. He never knew that his father had been killed. His father never knew that his child would follow him so soon in death.

Later that month, in the home of my brother, where I lived after our house was destroyed, I gave birth to a girl. I named her Mitsuyo, as her father had wished. Mitsuyo means light of the world, the light of peace. The light her father never saw.

Saving Them from Starvation

Tomiko Ukita

WE HAD FOUR CHILDREN. Our eldest daughter, a third-year primary school student at the time, had already been evacuated to Shimane Prefecture. The other three—a daughter in kindergarten, a three-year-old daughter, and an eight-month-old son—remained with us in Osaka. On the day of the air raid of March 13, 1945, our youngest daughter and our son both had measles. When the alarm sounded, I gathered them up and headed for the nearby air-raid shelter. As often happened, my husband, who was the head of a local neighborhood association, was too busy with official duties to be with us. Because I thought the alarm would be lifted soon, I took nothing with me except two blankets. But the alarm remained in effect throughout the night. The shelter became so filled with smoke that we could no longer breathe. I resolved to risk going outside.

Everything was a scorched wasteland. Our house was gone. I looked for my husband in hope that he had managed to salvage something. During the hours that followed, I hurried from place to place. I took temporary shelter in a surviving school building; and there the two blankets, the only possessions I had left in the world, were stolen from me. But none of us thought of crying or complaining. We were too happy to be alive.

As it began to rain, we returned to the smoldering, now steaming, ruins of our house. The frying pans and other pots that had not been destroyed had been pilfered by thieves. Our safe remained intact but was empty. Still, to this point, we were fortunate. My husband soon joined us. Though we had nothing, we had not been suffocated, as many people who took refuge in private shelters had been. Nor had we drowned or been scorched to death by swirling flames, as had been many people who fled to the rivers.

87

But from that time on, our lives were miserable. My husband could find no work. All six of us lived in the house of a relative until the situation became unbearable and we evacuated to Okayama Prefecture, west of Osaka. Not long afterward, however, we began to feel unhappy and alone there and returned to Osaka. Air raids continued to be severe around Higashiyodogawa Ward, where we lived.

My husband soon began suffering from stomach ulcers and anemia. He frequently vomited blood. I had just given birth to our fifth child; but six months later, leaving the baby in the care of our eldest daughter, I went to work.

I hated mealtimes. There was so little to offer the children. As they scrambled for whatever was available, my husband and I, though hungry, looked on and ate little. For diapers, I ripped the covers from our quilts. I was unable to repair our tattered clothes because we could not afford to buy needles and thread. Since we had no soap, baths were impossible. Our clothes were infested with lice.

I worked for a full month at a company that then went bankrupt, leaving me unpaid. Still my husband's health forbade his finding a job. I had to go on. For some time I was employed in a cotton mill, where I inhaled so much dust and fiber that I developed headaches and fevers. Then I went to work in a cement factory, where my face acquired a permanent coat of dust that would not come off, no matter how hard I scrubbed.

Finally I found a job at an American air base where the pay was better but the work much harder. I mowed grass all day under the scorching sun. But there was one good point about working there: the Americans discarded many things, like blankets, sheets, soap, shoes, and even meat, that I hid under my clothes when I went home in the evenings. I remember making overcoats for my children from the blankets. I worked at the base for two years and eight months and in this way saved my family from starvation.

Only a Few Months Longer

Sueko Mano

ON OUR WEDDING DAY, April 13, 1942, I was nineteen; and my husband was twenty-four. He wore his civilian-defense uniform; I had on the cotton *mompe* bloomers that women wore during the war.

Shortly after our wedding, we had a serious discussion of our immediate future. At that time, he was employed in the civil service. His salary was small, but it was guaranteed to be paid throughout his military service in the event he was drafted. He had been offered work in a munitions factory, where the salary was three times that of his present job. But because of the guarantee, we decided that he should stay with the civil service.

Eight months after our marriage my husband was operated on for appendicitis. His recuperation was slow, and a draft summons arrived before he was completely well. He was sent to the Twenty-second Battalion for three months' training as a reservist. After two months he was allowed to see his family. I had given birth to a child by then. Carrying the infant on my back, I joined my husband's parents in visiting him. In spite of restrictions against giving things to trainees, I made some small packets of his favorite foods and distributed them about my kimono and in the baby's clothes.

We talked for an hour on a bare plot of ground under the constant surveillance of one of my husband's superiors, who treated him like a criminal or a prisoner. One look told me that my husband had suffered under severe training. Clearly he was undernourished. His face looked as if he had been brutally beaten. I took out the food I had brought, and he gulped it down under the very eyes of his superior. He later wrote me that after the interview he was severely punished for this act of insubordination.

89

On April 24, 1944, he returned to us. We did not hide from each other our joy at his release; but we did not display it in front of others, because in those days everyone was so thoroughly indoctrinated by the militarists that our hatred of army life would certainly have been regarded as treachery.

Soon other men in our family were drafted. My two elder brothers and my brother-in-law were called. My brother-in-law, who owned a small farm, had eight children and was looking after his aged father. His summons was a heavy blow to the family, especially since the spring and summer are the busiest time for rice farmers. Without seeing my brother-in-law off, my husband and I hurried to the farm to be of assistance for a few days.

Shortly after supper one day after our return to Osaka from the farm, I went to close the front door and saw a messenger from the ward office not far away. He was walking with lantern in hand. "Maybe he's taking some poor man a draft notice," I thought. Then I was paralyzed with fear. He was heading in our direction.

The draft call was for my husband. This time, he was being sent to the front, to danger of death, and was to leave on May 5.

Only twenty-three and responsible for a baby only a little over a year old, I was confused and unhappy. My husband scolded me sharply when I wept on the night before his departure. "A soldier's wife must not cry," he told me. His words were so painful to me that I resolved not to weep the following morning.

While my mother-in-law was preparing breakfast on the morning he was to leave, something ominous happened. As she opened the bean-paste jar, the lid broke in half. Though we were both disturbed, we kept it from my husband.

Five other men from our neighborhood were drafted at the same time. At the sending-off ceremony held for them by the neighborhood association, my husband made a speech that nearly made me cry. But true to the oath I had made the preceding night, I restrained my tears. The ceremony ended; everyone started to go to the train station. My husband called me aside and asked me not to go. "If you are at the station, it will only make it harder for me." We parted. Though I did not dream it then, it was forever.

For two months I waited for letters that did not come. Then, one day the wife of another of the men drafted with my husband called on me to say she had met my husband, who had asked her to look me up. According to her, his unit had been sent to the front. She did not know their destination. I was hurt not to have been able to catch at least a glimpse of him before he left.

After the air raid of March 13, 1945, destroyed our home, we evacuated to the country; and I lost contact with the woman who had brought me the news, though I later heard that her husband had been killed in action.

The war ended. My brothers-in-law and my husband's friends were demobilized. Still there was no word of him. I listened to the missing-persons lists on the radio daily but never heard his name.

Several years after the war—sometime in 1949—I received official notification that he had died of illness in central China, on July 14, 1945. They sent me an unvarnished wooden box containing his ashes. For a long while, I went on believing that it was a mistake. The ashes were indistinguishable from any others. For me, my husband was alive. But gradually I gave in to the truth.

At the fine funeral held for him by the people of the village where he was born, I thought how short and empty his life had been. If he had lived only a few months longer, the war would have been over; and he would have received proper treatment.

Why Not Sooner?

Rie Kuniyasu

I WAS BORN DURING THE Meiji era (1868-1912), a time when people were taught to be loyal to the emperor and respectful to

91

parents. When the tide turned against Japan in the latter part of World War II, I worked hard in the hope of contributing to our ultimate victory. When my son Chuichi was drafted, I held back my tears. I did not tell him to come home safe. Soldiers were expected to be prepared to die honorably on the field of battle.

Just prior to his departure, we had a family photograph taken. When it was printed, my daughter and son were shown without heads. At the time, my husband and I did not let it upset us.

The March 13, 1945, air raid on Osaka destroyed both our house and our shop, leaving us without a place to live. But my brother-in-law found us a house in the fairly safe Yamato region. Living there, we were never alarmed by air raids.

On the morning of June 15, 1945, my daughter told me of a dream she had had the night before. She had been attacked by a B-29 and could not run away. She said the dream frightened her and made her want to stay home from work. I suggested that she do so; but she refused, saying that she had the key to the munitions-plant building where she worked and that she had to open up for the others.

She did not come home at the usual hour in the evening. When she had not returned by three o'clock in the morning, my husband and I went to the train station to look for her. Unable to find her, we decided to go to Osaka, where her factory was located. But the air raids had delayed the trains so that we were unable to leave until nine the next morning. When we finally reached the factory, at three o'clock in the afternoon, one of the girls who knew my daughter rushed to us and cried, "I can't tell you how sorry I am."

A B-29 flying overhead had dropped a bomb. It had fallen on my daughter before she had a chance to reach the air-raid shelter.

It had been just like her dream. Why had I not forced her to remain at home that day? Unable to believe that she was dead, I questioned the factory people over and over again. Then, in spite of my husband's scolding, I wept bitterly and long.

92

Not far away from the place where the factory held a fine funeral for my daughter, wooden boxes containing unidentified corpses were being burned. At least, my child had escaped that fate. Silently I said to her, "Wait a little while. We'll be with you soon."

Our son was at the front; our daughter, dead. We waited for the B-29s to kill us. But we lived. The war ended. When I heard the emperor's surrender message over the radio, I was filled with rage. Why had we not surrendered two months earlier? Then my daughter would have been spared.

Though day in and day out we waited in vain for news of our son, we still nurtured hope until, on the day of the ceremony marking the one hundredth day after our daughter's death, we read in the newspaper that his battalion had been destroyed in the Marianas. Several months later, we received official notification and a box containing a piece of wood on which was written his name. This was supposed to be his remains. Refusing to believe he was dead, I continued to look for him among the crowds of demobilized soldiers in the streets.

Then one day an army friend of his called to say, "Chuichi Kuniyasu died an honorable death shortly after the Americans landed on Saipan." At last I was able to give up hope.

My husband hid his grief, but soon his health began to deteriorate. He died in February, 1950.

Relieved That It Was Over

Tomie Akazawa

WE WANTED TO BE TOGETHER, even in death if necessary. That is why, when the air raids on the industrial districts in the

93

Kansai area intensified in 1945, we decided not to abandon our three-story house in Oyodo Ward, Osaka. My husband, I, and our teen-age daughter agreed to take our chances together.

After the severe American raid on Osaka, on March 13, 1945, our danger grew steadily greater. Watching the sky turn red from fires, we knew that our turn could not be far away. Sometimes, as we were awakened as often as five or six times a night by air raids, we even wished we might die if it would only end the anxiety.

One day in July, our district was raided. Everyone in our neighborhood fled either to the air-raid shelter or to a large water tank recently built on a plot of land from which the buildings had been razed. Incendiary bombs ignited buildings, houses, even the grass in vacant lots. The flames caused tremendous updrafts that lifted from our shoulders the quilts with which we tried to protect ourselves.

The horrible heat and the impenetrable smoke blackening the sky drove my husband frantic. He broke from us and threw himself into the water tank, where there were already countless refugees, some of them clinging to bicycles and even to live chickens.

My daughter was faint from the smoke. Suddenly her hood was in flames. I hastened to take it off, only to notice that my own was on fire. I tried to force my daughter to join her father in the water tank. My own strength was ebbing rapidly. I began to lose consciousness. Death seemed to be approaching. Then my daughter's screams woke me. Seeing that I was about to succumb, she called to me with all her might. In this way, she saved my life.

Finally, I lifted her into the water tank and dragged myself in after her. My husband ran away. He later thanked me over and over for saving our child and said that in times of great stress men are useless.

Those of us who managed to get into the water tank survived. People who sat in the field, beside their belongings, were burned together with the things they tried to protect. The head of our local neighborhood association was killed instantly by an incendiary bomb. My husband was wounded in the ankle by a flying fragment.

We had stored a large quantity of charcoal briquettes in our house as fuel for the coming winter. They fed the flames engulfing the building when the incendiaries hit. The house burned for two days and was completely destroyed. Nothing was left. But as luck would have it, my daughter's schoolteacher asked us to stay in his house until we found a place. We had stored some chests, cabinets, and other possessions in a safe place in nearby Sone. A few days after the raid we found a flea-infested room in which to live. We then hired a horse-drawn wagon to haul our chests to our new dwelling.

We had been wealthy before the war. Accustomed to maids, I never did heavy work. After the disastrous raid, however, my husband was incapacitated by the wound in his ankle, and I had to do everything. My arms bled internally when I lifted heavy objects. At one point, it became necessary for me to go to Sone to collect more of our belongings. On the way back, an air-raid alarm was sounded, and I was forced to flee to a shelter. Just as I was about to enter, a bomb exploded overhead, floating my body into the air. Miraculously I was spared; but after the raid was over I had to trudge along on foot with a heavy bag on my shoulder. The burden was too great. I stopped at one door to ask for help, but the wife of the house refused to speak to me. At the next door, I was more fortunate. A kind man agreed to keep my bag and gave me some bread — which was rationed then — and a cup of tea. I was deeply moved by his hospitality. At home, my husband and daughter waited in fear. They were convinced that my tardiness in returning meant I had been killed.

Somewhat later, kind friends whom my husband had helped before the war came with gifts of rice, barley, eggplants, cucumbers, and other food. I was very grateful.

When we heard the emperor's surrender message, I was not sorry that Japan had lost. I was only relieved that the war was over and that we were freed from much suffering.

95

CHAPTER THREE

Conflicting Fire

All Air seemd then
Conflicting Fire

JOHN MILTON
Paradise Lost, Book VI

When man wages war, slaughter and burning know no favorites. Fire pours from the sky, consuming everything below. There is no hiding place. The tongues of crimson flame lash all. They devour flesh and wood with equal greed and lap the surfaces of rivers to scorch and suffocate. When the flames expire, gray sooty men and women glide over the desolation to pick among burned beams and still-hot glass for the remains of loved ones. They then light small fires on which to burn the dead to ritual cleanliness. These lights bring back to dazed and weary eyes the chill terror of those hours when all air was conflicting fire.

March 10, 1945

Yoshiharu Matsue

IN THE LAST YEARS of World War II, my duty as fire warden was to scan the skies from the observation point on top of a primary school building and, on sighting enemy aircraft, which I had been trained to identify, to sound the alarm signaling the people of the district to take refuge in air-raid shelters. The Americans captured Saipan in July, 1944, and built there a large air base from which B-29s could make raids on the Japanese home islands. This turn in events stimulated the authorities to expand air-raid installations and to evacuate young schoolchildren from the city. The first bombs fell on Tokyo in November, 1944. By that time there were air-raid shelters throughout the city.

The B-29s usually bombed from very high altitudes. Taking off from the Mariana Islands, they flew toward Japan at from nine to ten thousand feet and used Mount Fuji as a primary landmark. Near the mountain, they veered right, dropped their bombs, and then headed south again. The raids intensified during February to reach a peak of massiveness and destructiveness on March 10, Japanese Army Day.

On March 9, the military authorities made a radio broadcast calling for the extermination of the Allies. During the early part of that evening there were two theories about the whereabouts of enemy aircraft. They were thought to be circling either off the southern tip of the Boso Pensinsula or over the sea off the Kujukuri beach. Both places are in Chiba Prefecture, adjacent to Tokyo.

Before long, announcement was made that the planes had left and were headed south. Relieved to hear this, I came down from my observation post and joined my family. Then suddenly we heard the roar of aircraft overhead. I hurried back to the observation post and sounded the alarm. Almost in the twinkling of an eye, as I looked on flabbergasted, the eastern part of the city burst into flames. The B-29s had abandoned their usual practice of high-altitude flying and had come in for the raid very low. This had made it impossible for me to identify them by the sounds of their engines.

Antiaircraft shells burst throughout the sky as searchlights picked out the underbellies of the huge planes. The raid was totally indiscriminate. The B-29s dropped cluster after cluster of cannisters, each containing dozens of projectiles that burst in midair and bathed everything below in flames. The heat of the fire that destroyed almost all our local school buildings was so intense that the glass in the windows melted. The tongues of flame are said to have been so high that fanned by the winds they were able to cross the Sumida River.

Following instructions given in mandatory training sessions, countless people perished as, engrossed in trying to put out the fires, they found themselves surrounded by the inferno. Most of the people who fled to the air-raid shelters suffocated. Realizing that such places were not safe, I led my mother to a primary school. Some people died in the building; but we escaped, narrowly.

Twice
Tomio Yoshida

THE FIRST THING WE did when we heard the alarm on March 9, 1945, was to gather our valuables and put them in one of the two air-raid shelters in the yard of our house, located in the eastern part of Tokyo. My elder sister quickly made balls of the rice she had been cooking, packed them in the rice cooker, and tied the cooker to her back. We told our parents to go at once to one of the two open areas in our neighborhood: Sarue Park or the lumberyard of the Ministry of Forestry. The two of us would join them later.

Shortly after they left, we heard the horrifying roar of the low-flying B-29s and the sound of incendiary bombs falling. The oily contents of the bombs oozed out, carrying flames to everything they touched. Water was no good in combatting the fire, and soon the groups of fire fighters threw aside their buckets and began trying to suffocate the flames with clothes and quilts. Nothing worked.

I snatched up a few of my prized belongings — my precious accordion (which I had bought with my small savings and which was the only solace available to me in the dark days of the war) was in the air-raid shelter, safe, I hoped. My sister and I went out into the street where strong winds fanned the fire and sent gusty showers of sparks falling on the heads of the countless people trying to flee to safety. Battling the powerful winds, we trudged to the edge of the park district but found the open space encircled by a ring of burning shops that made it impossible for us to enter. The lumberyard too was aflame. We did not know where to turn. After running about aimlessly for a while, we found a landing stage under a stone wall of one of the canals that crisscrossed our area. Two or three other people had already taken refuge there, and we joined them. Before long, there were thirty or forty of us.

Fierce winds spread the fire rapidly. My sister and I clung together, to encourage each other to endure the heat. Some kind person scooped water from the canal in a tin can and sprinkled it over us. After about two hours, during which we constantly trembled with fear of the roaring enemy aircraft and the rain of incendiaries, the fires in the north seemed suddenly to have burned themselves out. Then we began shivering with cold. Though my sister advised against it, I climbed to the top of the stone wall to try to warm myself at some embers still glowing there.

Jumping down again, I had begun walking toward my sister when I stepped on something squashy. I started to kick it aside but stopped abruptly. The burned thing lying on the landing stage was the first human corpse I had ever seen.

With dawn, we began to be very worried about our parents. We tried to go home but for a long time could not find the place. The neighborhood was a wasteland. Not a house remained in the formerly densely built-up region. Under a bridge we saw two dead women and two dead children, all charred beyond recognition.

Finally, we found the place where our house should have been. Nothing was left but ashes. The air-raid shelters had been destroyed. The one in which I had put my precious accordion had burned because of gasoline leaking into it from an automobile parked nearby. The automobile was still smoldering.

After a while, first mother then father returned. Though they could hardly see because smoke had caused their eyes to swell, they were otherwise unharmed. We had been right to urge them to evacuate early.

With no place to go, we squatted in the ruins of our home. In the afternoon another sister and her husband, who was a civilian employee of the army, came to see how we were. The house they lived in, in Mejiro, was still undamaged. They had been forced to walk part of the way to us because some of the train lines were wrecked. They told many horrible things about what they saw: corpses in mounds on the roads and dead bodies clogging the rivers.

Since none of us had eaten for a long time, we ate the rice balls my sister had prepared the night before and even had a few laughs at my recounting of her bravery during our ordeal by the canal.

We were all to stay with my elder sister for a while. To reach the train that would take us there, we had to walk through the ravaged area. The lumberyard of the Ministry of Forestry was still burning, as was a coal warehouse nearby. Dead bodies littered the streets. Some of the people who had tried to escape to the Sumida River had drowned; others had been trampled to death. Corpses with heads in the water or with arms outstretched as if in supplication for aid lay in piles on rafts in the river. Delicate plumes of incense drifted upward here and there where survivors were paying last respects to beloved dead.

On the western side of the Sumida River, damage was much less severe. When we finally reached Tokyo Central Station, we were allowed to board the train without tickets.

Seeing my home town ravaged in this way inspired me with patriotic zeal. I volunteered for military service soon after the March raid because I felt that in this way I could get even with the Americans and British, who, we had been taught, were nothing but devils and beasts.

After short tours of duty in various parts of Japan, I was sent to

Hiroshima. I was there when the atomic bomb fell. Because our unit had pitched camp under a bridge fairly far from the center of the city, I escaped injury. But I saw the havoc wrought by one hellish bomb. I had managed to live through the incendiary attack on Tokyo, but I would not have been so lucky if I had been in the heart of Hiroshima on that day.

Refugees fled from the city in all directions. I saw people burned from head to foot, eyeless, and grotesquely disfigured. A woman who had gone mad embraced a hot-water bottle as if it were an infant. Adhering to a crumbling concrete wall I saw a piece of a white medical coat. The only trace of the doctor who had worn it was a dark, rubberlike patch that had once been his head.

Very Little for So Much

Eiji Okugawa

I WAS A FUNNY-LOOKING soldier, hardly taller or heftier than the rifle issued to me. Until being drafted, in 1944, I had worked an exhausting schedule at an army arsenal. Just as all of us had tolerated the long work hours there without complaining, so all of us were determined to serve our country to the best of our abilities as new soldiers.

But army life was harsh. We were subjected to Spartan discipline. Drills were frightening. Any blunder earned a double slap in the face from the noncommissioned officers. When some of us did the noncoms' laundry to try to curry favor, we relieved tensions and frustrations by making fun of them behind their backs. We underlings trusted each other; we were all in the same boat and needed a way to let off steam. I recall one new recruit who, after being boxed on the ears for no apparent reason during roll

104

call, gave vent to his chagrin by having a long cry in the toilet.

As months passed, we began to hear disquieting rumors about the unfavorable way the war was beginning to go for Japan. One day a group of us piled into one of the charcoal-burning trucks used then because of the fuel shortage and went to haul a load of gravel from the bed of the Tama River. As we worked on the pebbly bank, a silver plane circled in the blue above us and began strafing. We scattered. But there was no cover in the open riverbed. Soon the plane flew away, but the air-raid signal sounded almost at once. The noncommissioned officer in charge of our detail ordered us back to the base. On the way we had to stop once, as an enemy plane flew over and dropped a bomb. We dashed under some trees. The shell landed nearby but did not explode.

Back at headquarters, everything was in confusion. Soldiers and officers dashed about the compound. The raid did no significant damage, but it was important for me. It was the first I had ever experienced. Still, according to official information bulletins — the only news we got — Japan was still winning.

On the following day, after maneuvers in a field pockmarked with dugouts, we were repeatedly strafed by enemy planes. We took cover in the dugouts, but the planes came back time and time again; they seemed to be increasing in number with each trip. And not a single Japanese aircraft offered them resistance. This happened in the fall of 1944.

Soon we heard disturbing hints that we were to be sent to the front. That meant probable death, and I did not want to die. Enemy raids increased to the extent that we were no longer fooled by the official bulletins. From early 1945, the American craft met no resistance at all except some ineffectual interceptor planes.

One night early in March, Tokyo underwent a horrendous, intensive incendiary raid. From our base on the outskirts we could see the entire eastern region of the city in flames. The sky was aglow. Antiaircraft guns had no effect against the B-29s. Soon

105

the fire spread in our direction. Our barracks caught. To fight the flames we had nothing but poles tipped with thick cotton rags that we dipped in water before smacking at the flames with them. I got out just before the whole barracks burst into flame and collapsed.

At dawn there was still a glow in the eastern sky from the fires. Our barracks lay in smoldering ruins. We had suffered some casualties, among them a close friend of mine, whom I missed very much.

Oddly enough, I distinctly remember the shape of the incendiary bombs. They were hexagonal in section, about fifty centimeters long, and about ten centimeters in diameter. Attached to them were blue, tapelike cords that caught on things as the bombs fell.

Only two weeks after we moved into new barracks, the building was engulfed in flames. I barely escaped once again. This time, immediately after the raid, I took leave to try to locate relatives and friends who had lived in the part of Tokyo that had suffered severely in the raid of March 9 and 10.

I could not find anyone. Their houses were destroyed. Everything was a scorched, pitted wasteland of ruins and charred bodies. Telephone poles had been either burned or uprooted. Once I had known this part of the city well. Now all the landmarks were gone. I could recognize very little, and all my efforts to locate friends and relatives proved fruitless.

Air raids on Tokyo continued, and then in August came Hiroshima and Nagasaki.

When I was discharged from the army, I received as a reward for my years of service to the country a handful of rice, some clothes, and the dim outlook of the uncertain postwar years.

What Condolences?

Aiko Matani

FOR A LONG TIME, the radio told us only how well things were going for our side; then, with increasing frequency, it began to report enemy aircraft in the skies over the Japanese home islands. My first recollection of direct contact with the enemy was seeing vapor trails—not the planes themselves—high in a blue sky. The authorities were taking steps for our safety. Children—including one of my sisters and my young brother—were evacuated to rural areas. Buildings were razed to widen fire lanes.

On March 9, 1945, my family closed the public bathhouse we operated early. A little after nine in the evening, we heard simultaneously the air-raid alarm and an explosion. Then another and another. Incendiary bombs showered down on our neighborhood. For a time, all of us assumed our assigned fire-fighting posts. But before long, my father ordered us to evacuate. Leading the way, he held one of my younger sisters and my mother by the hand. I carried my baby sister on my back. My older sister was nowhere to be seen.

As we fled, a flare revealed B-29s flying in huge formations at very low altitudes. I had heard that the planes were big; but seen from so close, their size astounded me. We saw injured and dying people all along the way. A barber's son whom I knew had an arm ripped off. Still we hurried on.

On the way to the school ground designated a safety zone, I suddenly felt intense heat at my waist. Looking down, I saw flaming boots on the feet of my small sister, who was on my back. As my parents disappeared into the smoke-obscured distance, I hastened to put the child down and pull the burning boots from her feet. Soon I caught up with my parents as we rushed into the school auditorium, which was already packed with refugees.

107

Then the doors were closed. Latecomers, no matter how they pleaded, were shut out. Steeling our hearts against pity, we refused to open the doors for fear the flames would suddenly be sucked into the room. My family was near the entrance. Mother suddenly began screaming that my elder sister was still not with us. Then she sobbed and cried wildly. Nearly hysterical with fear myself, I brutally commanded her to shut up. I had never spoken to her in such a way before.

Through the windows we saw people near the building bathed in earthward-falling curtains of sparks. Then we could see them no more, for men in the auditorium were pressing straw mats against the windows in the vain hope of keeping out flames and sparks.

Suddenly fire shot up on all sides; an incendiary bomb had made a direct hit on the building. The fire warden at once ordered us to flee. But we could only hurl ourselves from the flames roaring inside into others roaring outside.

My father said we should make a break for a nearby park. We followed him. Nearby a woman with flaming hair rolled on the ground. A man ripped the blazing clothes from his body as he ran. Telephone poles were aflame, and strong north winds tossed sheets of corrugated iron and other heavy objects about the streets.

At the Yonnohashi Bridge it became apparent that we could not reach the park, since all roads leading to it were ablaze. But under the bridge itself, we found relative safety till morning, when, finally, after a long night of waiting, with soot-covered faces and smoke-swollen eyes, we began stumbling toward the place that had been home.

As we passed through the ruined town, we asked everyone we encountered about my sister. No one knew anything about her. Then, to our intense joy, we saw her trudging wearily not far in front of us. She carried a wrapping cloth containing three magazines and some clothes. In those times, everything was valuable.

The clothes, obviously, were of use; the magazines were employed in the toilet. Paper was very scarce.

Finding our house in ruins and learning that a neighborhood motion-picture theater was the safety shelter for our region, we put up a sign on our land, reading "All safe," and proceeded on our way.

I wept to see a burned mother and infant lying on the ground. At the theater, another mother was about to give birth. We did not know whether to congratulate or pity her.

We expressed happiness at the safety of neighbors who had survived. We mourned for those who had not; there were many of them. In a few days, my father, who was president of the local association of bathhouse proprietors, made rounds throughout the district and learned that a large number of our acquaintances and customers had perished. My elder sister and I too made calls, offering condolences where we could. But what could we say to bereaved survivors forced to dig holes to bury or to build pyres to cremate the remains of the innocent, beloved victims?

The Luckier
Tsuta Kawai

BEFORE THE WAR, my family operated an ice dealership. A summer of good business provided sufficient funds for us to live comfortably for three years. We had accumulated a considerable fortune and had built a large, handsome house. Not content to live in idle luxury, I devoted myself to the aid of less fortunate people. I served on various patriotic and social committees and helped take care of a large group of members of our neighborhood association.

109

After the war started and times became hard, I continued my charitable work. We were ordered to move from our comfortable house into a smaller one nearby. My family home was in Chiba Prefecture. When food became short, I took members of the neighborhood association to my family home, were there was always a good supply of rice and other foodstuffs. My mother invariably both fed the guests and prepared food for them to take back to Tokyo.

I made trips into nearby rural areas to procure fruit, vegetables, and pickles for the poor and received and distributed food sent to me by train from more distant regions. I was very close to all the people I tried to help. We were like a big family.

On March 9, 1945, I made another of many trips to the army officers' headquarters in Otsuka to try to convince the people there that his weak condition warranted a discharge for my husband, who had been called to service at a military installation. Since the next day was a holiday, my husband was permitted to return home for a while. On the way, we discussed the arrangements that would have to be made after his discharge.

At home we found our son, who had been doing research at the Ministry of the Navy, packing. He was to be called to the military soon. My husband returned to Otsuka in the early evening.

I went to a public bath and returned at about nine at night. The air-raid alarm was sounding. I disliked the bloomerlike *mompe* that women were supposed to wear in those days and never put them on except during air raids. I put them on that night. A strong wind contributed to an uncanny fear, unlike anything I had known before. The sirens seemed so shrill and persistent that I tried to make my son get out of bed. But insisting that it was probably just another false alarm, he turned over and tried to go to sleep.

Still the noise and commotion grew. From around the edges of the blackout curtains, I saw a reddish light. At last, unable to stand it any longer, I pulled the covers off my son and forced him

110

to get up. He had no combat experience, and what he saw when he drew back the curtains and opened the windows horrified him. The neighborhood not far away was a sea of flames. Stunned and dazed, he turned white and began trembling. Then he began scurrying about aimlessly. Next he pulled a hose into the room and began dousing everything with water, shouting to me wildly, "Mother, calm down. It's going to be all right."

I was calm enough. Seeing that there was no hope of saving the house, I packed up some valuables and dragged my son from the endangered building. He was so frightened that he forgot to dress; all he had on was trousers.

First we hurried to our former house. The building had a large basement, where we kept the rice and sakè for the farewell party we would give when our son left for the military. I deposited the valuables in the basement, and we left at once for the Seikosha Building, which housed a company owned by friends of the family. They had told us that in time of disaster we should come to their building to take refuge in their asolutely safe basement.

When we arrived, we found the basement packed with people. My son, who had regained his composure, saw at once that this was no place for us. If the building should catch fire, everyone in the basement would be roasted. We left and headed for the Gonohashi area, where we hoped to find shelter. On the way, we encountered a man pulling a cart filled with bedding. My son suddenly saw that the bedding had caught fire and that there were three children wrapped in it. Screaming for the man to stop, my son rescued the children and hurled the burning quilts from the cart. In a short time, the man had rearranged his belongings and his children and was off again, having received advice from my son to be more careful of his offspring in the future.

The Gonohashi area was already an inferno. We had to turn back and fight our way among the crowds of refugees thronging the streets. My son held my hand tightly so that we would not be separated. Hurrying past the company of our family friends, we reached our former home. By this time, I was so tired and wretched that I wanted to go into the house and stay. But my son, who was now in better command of the situation than I, argued that soon the fire would sweep over this area too. Our beautiful, expensive home. Why did it have to burn? What had any of us done to deserve this?

My son pulled me away, weeping, from the house and led me to the eastern part of Kameido, where the fires had started but had already largely burned themselves out. We sat down by the smoldering ruins of what had been a fire station and waited. Before long, someone shouted, "Look! The Seikosha Building's on fire." Turning that way, we saw smoke and flames billowing from the windows. Our former home too was now doomed. Clinging to my son, I sobbed, "I don't care what happens now, as long as we are together."

At five thirty in the morning, a large, red sun rose through the clouds of smoke over the blackened ruins and the charred corpses. With the sun to our back, we started walking home. But we no longer had any home. Both of our houses had been destroyed. Our basement and all the valuable food stored in it were no more. I heard that the people who had taken refuge in the basement of the Seikosha Building had all been suffocated to death. As we stood in front of the smoking rubble that had been our home, a neighbor hurried to us and asked in a trembling voice whether we had seen her husband. We could do nothing to comfort or help her.

As a result of that one air raid, our neighborhood association was reduced from thirty-eight to eight members. I do not know how the victims died. Perhaps in trying to save their loved ones or their property. My son, my husband, and I survived. Although I lost a brother-in-law, a younger brother, and cousins in the war, I suppose we were among the luckier ones.

The Day Off
Yoshimitsu Mano

UNDER ORDINARY CIRCUMSTANCES, I would have been at work on the night of March 9, 1945; but I was at home because I had taken the day off to forage for food. At midnight, when the B-29s started roaring overhead, we left our house. My wife carried our infant son on her back, and I carried our five-year-old son wrapped in a summer quilt. We dashed about in search of safety in the raging fires till we found ourselves on a river embankment. Flames licked the slope we had just climbed, and only the water offered a chance of escape.

Floating not far from the shore was a raft. I told my wife that I would leap in first and that she was to follow when I called and told her the raft was safe. Carrying my son on my back, I jumped toward the raft but slipped and got caught between two logs. After I flailed about for a while, I managed to climb onto the raft. Though I called to her at the top of my lungs, my wife did not answer. Nowhere against the red of the sky could I see either her or my infant son.

Before long the two of us on the raft were showered with hot, dangerous sparks. Time and time again, I dipped the summer quilt into the river and covered our heads and shoulders with it, only to have to wet it soon: the heat dried it out quickly.

Then the flames died down. But the north wind began to blow. Drowsiness was our next lethal enemy. If we slept, we would die of cold and exposure. I stayed awake, but I had to slap my boy frequently to keep him from dropping off. At dawn, after a long night, I called to someone on the bank, who pulled us ashore.

We had no home to go to. Among the horrifying mounds of charred, unrecognizable bodies, we stumbled away from the river,

113

fearing that my wife and younger child might be among the dead. After a kind person gave us some rice, we went to the house of a friend in Kameido. We trudged through the silent wasteland of burned buildings and corpses only to find my friend's house destroyed. Then I decided to go to the home of some relatives. It was a long way, and to find trains still running we had to walk all the way to Ichikawa Station. When we finally got there, as bomb victims, we were allowed free rides to our destination. Our relatives took us in; and for days I traveled into the bombed area, trying to locate my lost loved ones. Finally I gave them up.

Fifteen days after the bombing, I took my surviving son to our neighborhood to hold a memorial service and burn incense. By chance, during our prayers, I spied a familiar-looking hood of the kind women wore during air raids in those days. I picked it up. It was hers. I found it on the embankment where I had last seen them alive.

Searching frantically, at length I found them in the mud near the water's edge. The child was still strapped to my wife's back. They had been in the water for more than two weeks.

After recovering the bodies, I went for the person who had been the go-between in our wedding and for some relatives. After we made a definite identification, we placed the bodies on an iron sheet set on two stones. It took all day to cremate the bodies with logs and whatever scraps of wood we could find.

Later I carried their ashes to a temple in our home prefecture, Ibaraki. If I had not taken March 9, 1945, off, I might have been unable to save even one child from the flames.

Death and Birth in the Flames

Masayoshi Nakagawa

BY MARCH 9, 1945, my wife, my eldest son (two years old), my second daughter (six), and I had been running from air raids for weeks on end. My wife, who was about to give birth, had at last been put in a hospital in a part of Tokyo called Kinshicho. Our other two children had been evacuated to a rural area for safety. On that night, my son and daughter and I had been asleep in our home near the Tokyo Gas Company for some time when, once again, the air-raid alarms and the shrieks and cries of fleeing people split the calm. By the time I was able to get out of bed, the neighborhood had been hit. The entire night sky was aflame. Enemy aircraft continued to drop incendiary bombs, as unusual, tricky winds fanned the fires and churned up whirlwinds of smoke and black dust.

My daughter did her best to help pack what we could. Then she took my bundle, as I strapped my son to my back and tried to carry the emergency kit we kept ready. The three of us dashed out into the panic and pandemonium of the streets. People were carrying whatever they had managed to salvage: quilts, pillows, frying pans. Some of them had carts; others lugged bicycles on their backs. I realized at once that I would have to abandon the emergency kit if I was to carry my boy through the crowd. The flames were closing in.

Trying to run, but forced by heat and wind to stumble, we pushed our way through the mob, even sometimes trampling on other people in our desperation to reach the safety of the open space between the Onagi River and the tanks of the Tokyo Gas Company — fortunately empty at the time.

Suddenly I heard a shout: "Your son's clothes are on fire!" At the same instant, I saw flames licking the cotton bloomers my

115

daughter was wearing. I put my son down and reached out to try to smother the flames on his back when a tremendous gust of wind literally tore me from him and threw me to the ground. Struggling to stand, I saw that I was now closer to my daughter than to the boy. I decided to put out the fire on her clothes first. The flames were climbing her legs. As I frantically extinguished the flames, I heard the agonized screams of my son a short distance away. As soon as my daughter was safe, I rushed to the boy. He had stopped crying. I bent over him. He was already dead.

But there was no time to stop. I lifted him to my back and, taking my daughter's hand, ran from the ever-pursuing inferno. Once in the open space by the gas tanks, I stood, my daughter by my side, my dead son in my arms, waiting for the fire to subside.

In the light of dawn, I saw total ruin where our neighborhood had been. Knowing that our house too was gone, like the rest, I decided to go to the home of a relative. My daughter and I, hand in hand, alone now, started off. Weary and emotionally drained, we had to force ourselves to struggle on through mounds of debris and corpses; among the foul, pungent odors; and amid the groans of the injured and dying. A man holding a frying pan gazed blankly at ashes that had been a house. Another squatted, dazed and helpless, in the middle of the street. Mothers frantically called for their children; small children screamed for their parents. I neither could nor wanted to do anything for the suffering people around me. My own suffering was too great. Probably all the others felt the same way.

Near the Kameido railway station, mounds of bodies clogged the track underpass. The walls were spattered with blood. A charred mother sat embracing her charred infant. The dead, burned beyond recognition, looked like grotesque, bald dressmaker's dummies. Those who were still alive moaned against the heat and called for water.

Many people had jumped into the river and clung to logs or other floating debris. But they were suffocated when drafts brought great tongues of flame sweeping along the surface of the water. Some few survived by pouring water over themselves or by jumping into specially constructed emergency water tanks. Although my son had been killed, it was miraculous that even my daughter and I had escaped.

On March 9, the day of the horrible attack, my wife gave birth to a girl. The hospital too had been bombed with incendiaries, and she had been forced — weak as she was — to flee for safety with her newborn child in her arms. She had asked someone to take the baby to a safe place but had been advised curtly to abandon the child: it would be a burden to her. But she could not bring herself to follow this counsel and fled into the flames unassisted. At a swimming pool in Kinshicho, she stopped to pour water over herself and the baby. In this way, she saved both lives from the showers of sparks through which she had to pass.

The morning after the raid, she returned to the ruins that had been our house. No one she met knew anything of our whereabouts. The only thing she could think to do was to make the long trip on foot to the home of some relatives. Her delivery had been difficult. She was exhausted. Finally, unable to go on farther, she sat down in the middle of the street. A kind passerby noticed her condition and took her to a hospital.

Shortly after my daughter and I had reached the relatives' home where we were to take refuge, I set out to try to trace my wife. I went to the maternity hospital in Kinshicho and found it destroyed. All my searching proved vain. After praying for days that she and the infant were safe, I had come to the conclusion that I had lost them, as I had lost my small son. Then I received a telegram telling me that she and the baby were safe. I was overjoyed. Our experiences had been shattering, but we were more fortunate than countless others.

Who Is To Blame?

Nisaku Kokubu

LIKE MOST JAPANESE at the time, I was very patriotic during World War II; but my work in a food-rationing center — located in my house — exempted me from military service. In Fukugawa, Tokyo, where I lived, food was growing very short by March, 1945. In those days, rice, fish, and vegetables were rationed. To stretch our food as far as possible, I sometimes mixed millet, bean cake, and even common grass with rice. I made and distributed bean-paste soup without vegetables or any other additional ingredients. To provide as much assistance and food as possible to the people of our district, we worked day and night.

It was a cold, snowy winter. In February, the American air raids on Tokyo intensified. Kanda, Miyoshi, and Tategawa suffered heavy damage. But our house, located near Tategawa, had escaped. Though we were slightly apprehensive at the turn events were taking, we felt that our efforts would inevitably result in Japanese victory. But still, the air-raid alarm, sounding at all hours of the day and night, got on our nerves.

As time passed, however, we grew somewhat accustomed to both the raids and the alarms. When an air raid was signaled at eight in the evening of March 9, most of us were undisturbed and even muttered, "Not again!" as we put up our blackout curtains. My wife and four children were with me in the rationing office. After making necessary preparations, we went on with the work of sorting cards for still undelivered rice supplies. Nothing happened for a long time. My family and I shared a muffled laugh at the thought that the Americans might just be teasing this time. At midnight B-29s roared overhead. I thought it was strange: we had heard no further alarms since the one at eight o'clock.

Suddenly, around the edges of the curtains we could see a light almost as bright as day. I hurried outside. Planes were drop-

118

ping showers of incendiary bombs. One of them hit a house two or three doors from ours. The building instantly burst into flame. A bucket brigade quickly formed. Someone called me to help.

At that moment another incendiary fell in the backyard of my own house. "I can't help now. My house's on fire too!" I shouted as I ran indoors to find my wife putting out the fire with water from an emergency tank in the yard. But sparks fell like rain, and I knew that we could not stay there. Houses were catching fire one after the other all around us.

"We're getting out of here!" I called to my wife and children. "Let's go to the burned-out area in Tategawa. We'll be safe there."

Packing a small cart with essentials, we set out. My wife had the youngest child strapped to her back and held the hands of two others. Our eldest daughter, who was eighteen, pushed the cart. About fifty meters from our house, my wife remembered that she had not brought the rice cooker and a frying pan. These were necessities. I went back into the rain of sparks for them.

After I returned to the group, we set out together again. This time, a gust of wind whipping past nearly swept us from our feet and overturned the cart. In the twinkling of an eye, the rice bag split open; and a great deal of rice spilled on the ground. My wife and daughter started scraping it up, but they irritated me by being so slow. I pushed them aside and scooped up most of the spilled grain. Standing and gripping the handle of the cart, I said, "Let's go."

There was no answer. Turning, I was dismayed to find that my wife and three of our children had disappeared. They had been behind me during the thirty seconds I had taken to scoop up the rice. My eldest daughter had been so busy rearranging things on the cart that she had not noticed. Now they were gone. Where? I screamed for them wildly. No answer. The houses in the neighborhood were being engulfed in flames. Fleeing people packed the street.

Forced to give up our search for the time being, my daughter

119

and I joined the stream of refugees trudging helplessly among the devouring flames and through the stench of the charred bodies scattered along the road. Still the planes mercilessly hurled down their infernal incendiaries.

After a sleepless night, my daughter and I resumed our search. One by one, we examined the corpses lying in heaps by the rivers, in the parks, in the schoolyards, and on bridges. In the beginning, the bodies frightened and nauseated us; then we got used to them.

For days we wandered lamely about, looking everywhere and checking lists of the dead posted in police stations and in ward offices. All our efforts proved futile. Finally we gave up.

Shortly after the war, the strain of our experiences proved too great for my daughter. Constitutionally weak, she contracted and died of tuberculosis, leaving me with a six-year-old son, who had been evacuated to safety in the country with other students from his primary school.

Who is to blame for the loss of my wife and children? The United States? Japan? At first, I cursed the Japanese military for waging a hopeless war and bringing death to innocent people. I have now come to see that it is not only Japan and the United States who were at fault. War itself is the evil, and all those who would wage it must be held culpable.

A Plea
Tai Kitamura

ON JANUARY 13, 1945 — a dull, cloudy day — just before stepping into the shelter when the air-raid alarm sounded, I said a few words to one of my neighbors. In the next instant, he was hit by a bomb.

120

When the raid was over, I went out of the shelter to find his head on the ground. I nearly fainted. But then I recalled my duty as a human being and began collecting the parts of his dismembered body, which were scattered over about three hundred meters. As I went through this horrible task, I was suddenly struck with the terrifying thought that perhaps someday soon someone would have to do the same thing for me.

On March 9, 1945, I took refuge in a shelter at the end of a large, grassy field near my house. The American planes first dropped something greasy and then incendiary bombs, which ignited the oily substance and sent fires racing madly through the neighborhood. Strong north winds fanned the flames. Later I learned that the Americans had counted on this kind of weather condition.

Inside the air-raid shelter, I almost immediately lost consciousness. When I woke up, I could not open my eyes because of the soot and ashes that filled the air. Gradually, however, I came to see. Dead bodies were heaped in the cramped space. Some of them seemed glued together by their burns.

Today I live in peace with my children and grandchildren. Sometimes I almost forget the horrors of the war. But they must not be forgotten. And I have written this little note as a plea to the younger generations. They must know what war is like and must do all within their power to see that it never plagues the earth again.

CHAPTER FOUR

The Longing
To Return

Do you not see the young men
Going to the frontiers?
Probably they will never return.
Day and night
    they will long for a letter.
But the rivers and mountain passes
    will always dash their hopes.

·   ·   ·

O, the youthful faces,
    have they changed?
Will barbarian horses trample them to death?
Will they escape to be reunited with their families?

PAO CHAO
"The Tedious Ways"

When man wages war, young and old must quit homes for alien ground, perhaps to leave their bones and final blood drops there. When they fall, what is on their lips? No mention of the cause then. Only last pleas for mother, wife, child. Neither high-sounding slogans nor historic necessity brings solace to the man alone in steaming jungle or frozen tundra, the man consumed by the need to survive to satisfy the longing to return.

From a Soldier's Diary
Kiyoharu Tanno

AT THE END of September, 1943 we were ordered to get ready to take part in a punitive mission. Preparation, involving weapons, horse harnessing, ammunition, and food for human beings and animals, has put everyone in the camp in a tremendous bustle. But we have not been told at what time we are to assemble. I am to go along as a medic. It will be my first combat experience.

At about eight o'clock in the evening, after mess, we were mustered in the company square and told that we were to march from Ching-chou to Pa-ling-shan, slightly to the north. A Chinese outfit has been using this area as a base for nighttime raids on the district controlled by our Second Battalion. Pa-ling-shan is a treeless mountain, at the foot of which is a town, where the Chi-

125

nese outfit masquerades as merchants during the day and attacks at night.

Our forces, including a company of machine guns and a small artillery outfit, surrounded Pa-ling-shan about one hour before daybreak. We had no idea what the situation in the town was.

The enemy was completely surrounded. At dawn, headquarters gave the order; and the battle trumpet sounded from the sixth company. At the same time, artillery opened fire. The members of the Chinese outfit, taken by surprise, resisted for about twenty minutes and then ran as fast as they could. In the first light, we could see them dashing from the town across the fields and hills. The punitive expedition was over, and our company entered the town from the west. The fifth, sixth, and seventh companies were there ahead of us. Our orders from headquarters were to prepare mess and wait for further instruction.

For a few minutes I wandered around at a loss. Then one of my buddies called out, "Hey, Tanno. Give me a hand!" He was beginning to enter a house to commandeer whatever rice, salt, or other foodstuffs he could find. I was supposed to help him carry his plunder. Soldiers from all the other companies were doing the same thing.

My buddy ordered a man to come out of the house by calling in Chinese, "Lai-lai!" The man answered something that I did not understand and surrendered. We took him to our company. The same thing happened several times. In thirty minutes we had taken five prisoners this way. Then, smashing doors, furniture, and whatever we found for fuel, we built fires and cooked.

This punitive expedition has been a series of surprises for me. It was my first taste of the murderous part of military life.

> Dressed in holiday clothes,
> A Chinese girl
> Flees from death.

Since about the tenth of October, rumors of a big battle have

126

been flying around the company. Everybody has been busy getting ready. On the thirteenth, the list of people to participate in the operation was issued. I am to go along as a medic again.

On the fifteenth, we left Ching-chou and bivouacked that night at a town called Sha-shih. On the following day, weapons, munitions, and supplies were issued.

At about three o'clock in the afternoon, our company crossed the Yangtze and began days and days of sleeping out doors and of forced marching westward through a land of seemingly endless, flat plains.

For a week since we left Ching-chou we have been in flat land. The sky is clear, and the moon at night is bright. Good conditions for marching. In all the regions we cross, the harvest has just been taken in. There is no shortage of rice.

On the afternoon of the eighth day out, heavy drops of rain began to fall; and the weather turned cold. We were all very tired.

Hoping for rest that night, we plodded on. The rain developed into a downpour. Then we began hearing shots. The old troopers hoped for some strong fighting from the Chinese. The forward companies were already in battle readiness.

We stopped, and a violent exchange of fire started. This was another first for me, another of a long series of shocks for which I have not been prepared. I dashed into a nearby riverbed and lay down to escape enemy bullets. But the old-timers nonchalantly dug sweet potatoes in a field. They called me to help. Baked sweet potatoes for supper! But my arms and legs were trembling so badly that I could not stand.

The fighting continued after dark. With superior knowledge of the terrain, the enemy took up positions on the hills, from which they opened steady fire on us as we moved along the valley.

I was wet, cold, trembling, and frightened of the outcome of my first major encounter. My buddies jeer at me, and I try to put up as brave a front as possible.

127

As my buddies fall,
What joy for me?
Only grief as the fighting goes on.

Four in the morning, May 27, 1945. Our company has been ordered to march into the mountains beyond Yo-chou. Rain, day in day out. I have on a raincoat, and a protector hangs from my hat to my shoulders; but from the waist down I am sodden. Even through the mud, we continue our forced march. All the streams we have to ford are swollen. Water leaks into everything; back packs, mess kits, gear bags. But it is my responsibility to keep the medicine kit dry and to protect it at all costs. The lives of the men in the company depend on what is in that kit.

The rice seedlings have already been planted in the paddies.

On our long way through the mountains, we have encountered minor skirmishes but have pushed on toward Chang-sha beyond the Wan-yang mountains. Our horses were forced to go through passes barely wide enough for a human being. Meanwhile, the enemy rained bullets down on us. We must reach our goal, the town of Chang-sha.

The weather has cleared, and marching is easier. But now the companies ahead of us have been slowed down by the steep incline of the path. We have a chance to rest.

We started again soon. This time, up the nine hundred stone steps leading to the top of the mountain. On the way, we saw a monument to the defeat of the Japanese in the first battle of Chang-sha. After we reach the peak we still have a long way to go. Mountains of dead bodies are piled up on both sides of our road.

The result of all my efforts to this point has been a case of malaria. I have been running a high temperature for three days, but I must keep going. If I drop behind, it will be all over with me.

Endurance is proof
Of life continuing, even under
The chiseling ticking of my comrade's watch.

128

I have prayed to every god I know that the fever will go down. The company commander does not scold me; he looks on in silence as I take medicine and keep trying. In spite of my sickness, as a rookie soldier I am kept on mess detail. While suffering all this, I hear rumors of the occupation of Chang-sha.

June 25. No moon. The enemy thought they had cut us off, but we continued to move forward in the pitchy darkness. Men and horses frequently fall into paddies, streams, and creeks. Often the horses drown. Still, we have managed to get around the enemy and attack from the rear.

The enemy was in confusion. Our troops broke into one house after another and knifed the soldiers they found there. The startled Chinese fled to fields, roads, and even rooftops. In no time, without our having exchanged any fire, the enemy was wiped out.

The fighting stopped at dawn. We took a short rest to observe conditions. Some of us went toward a nearby farmhouse to look for something to use in preparing food. Suddenly a hand grenade was hurled out. "The enemy!" someone shouted. And we started hand-to-hand fighting with a group of Chinese. Fortunately, they were unarmed; and the hand grenade had been only a wooden dummy. One by one, we knifed the men. The skirmish ended together with their cries. They had been about thirty people who, unable to flee when we encircled their position, had taken cover in the farmhouse.

Some of the Chinese soldiers who fled to the fields were captured. Most of them were either shot or killed in hand-to-hand combat. Their bodies are piled up in mountainous heaps.

Though only a medic, I must kill too in order to protect myself.

In a foraging mission, some of our troops found what looked like pure, clear vegetable oil. They brought it back to camp, where it was used to make tempura. People of weak constitution who ate the tempura began to suffer acute stomach pains about one hour after the meal. It took from two to three hours to make stronger men sick. The oil had been some kind of machine lubricant and was harmful. The sick men came to us medics for help. Of course, we did what we could for them; but in practically no time, the order to move out came.

Then diarrhea struck. We all wore loin cloths made of a white, Chinese fabric. As these became soiled during the march because of the sickness, the men began to suffer from chafed, irritated groins, which made walking extremely painful.

After a day or two, some of the men recovered; but others got worse. They fell victims to a bloody flux that was diagnosed as amebic dysentery.

For four months, we have trudged about Sha-shih and Hu-nan provinces. In that time, many of my comrades have died. I have resolved to survive. I want to go home to see my family, at least once more. But the chances of going home soon are slim. No one gets sent back for good.

People come and go. Right now there are about five hundred names on our outfit roster. But most of them have died in battle, are in the hospital, or are missing. There are only about one hundred and fifty or two hundred of us still in fighting condition.

Home is a long way in the future. All we can do is go on fighting and win, win, win. We are no longer ordinary human beings. We are wild animals, barbarians, who sleep outside every night and who kill whatever we find for food.

Suffer, Suffer, Then Die
Kihei Matsumura

NOW WHEN I come home from work, my grandchild welcomes me with a loud, cheerful laugh. As I sit resting, I reflect that if it had not been for the nightmare of war some thirty years ago my

130

elder brother and many of my friends would still be alive and would be able to see and play with this charming child.

On March 3, 1944, when Japan was already fighting a losing battle, I was drafted into the Tokushima Thirty-third Regiment of the Japanese army. My brother had been drafted a little earlier. On July 7, after three months of harsh training, we shipped out for the south. As our transport sailed away, I realized that I had little hope of returning to Japan alive and regretted having spent my youth working hard to support our poverty-stricken family. I was twenty-one at the time.

We landed at Singapore, traveled to Bangkok, and from there took a train to Burma. Uneasy in a foreign land, for the first time in my life I realized how dear home was.

In December we were to have joined the One Hundred and Forty-third Regiment as reinforcements but were suddenly re-assigned to the Mori Special Raiders. This was tantamount to a death sentence, since the Mori Raiders were little more than bait, expendables in the protection of the other troops. The first thing we did was set out on a hellish basic-training course in guerrilla-style combat. Japanese forces had already lost control of the air. Our commander was killed in the fighting, and the deputy commander lost a leg. Though forced to walk with a crutch, he still participated in diversion missions. We hid by day and attacked by night.

We were expected to suffer, suffer, and then die. Originally there were about fourteen hundred men in my outfit. In a single battle, half of them would be killed; then replacement troops would be called in from other units.

In the many battles that took place in and around Moulmein, when ordered to forage for food, we raided villages and killed people. During the rainy season, we waded for days on end in water. Grass and pieces of wood were food for us. One after another, countless of my comrades sank into the swamps, dead of malnutrition, malaria, or enemy gunfire. Most of them called for their mothers or murmured the names of their wives and children. The wounded who were unable to keep up with us were ordered to commit suicide. If they refused, they were shot.

In Japan, the war was over on August 15, 1945. At that time, I was still fighting in Rangoon. We had seen leaflets and heard radio broadcasts announcing surrender, but none of us believed it. Finally, on September 14, when surrounded by enemy troops, we definitely learned of the defeat. There were forty-eight of us remaining alive from an original fourteen hundred.

When I at last reached Japan, I found a land charred and wasted by the fires of war. Prices of everything were steadily rising, and the poverty of my family was more dire than it had been. I suffered a relapse of malaria contracted in Burma; and as a result of malnutrition, cataracts developed on my eyes. Mine was only some of the suffering and loss inflicted on ordinary people because of a war undertaken by a group of Japanese military leaders.

Not Just Fighting and Bullets

Shoichi Kawano

IN AUGUST, 1937, when we were sent to Shanghai, I was in charge of baggage for the Tokushima Forty-third Regiment. Ten days after landing, we fought in a battle so fierce that half the men in our outfit were killed. Corpses from both sides lay everywhere. Maggots fed on the flesh of the dead. A creek was so filled with the bodies of Japanese soldiers that water barely showed at all. The stench of death hung heavy in the air.

Over and over, I told myself, "This is the way war is, but I don't want to die. I want to live, even for this one day."

War is not just a matter of fighting and bullets. Soldiers must battle hunger, malaria, dysentery, and cholera. For days, we had no time to take off our shoes. When we did remove them, they would fall apart; and the stench of dirty socks and maggots would sicken us. Sometimes, I traded shoes and socks with freshly killed corpses. Of course, no one had time to think of laundry. To cook rice we used water from the streams. The grease of human flesh floated on the surface. But we did not dare take water from wells, which the enemy might have poisoned or polluted with bacteria. For a long time, I could not get out of my mind the comment a buddy let slip: "Why and for whose sake do I have to suffer and fight this way?"

In the desperation of war, men cease being human. Pillage, arson, and murder are everyday affairs. The soldier unhesitatingly shoots mother and child who, with hands joined in supplication, beg to be spared. He even stops thinking about his own sad, miserable life, for he too may die in a few minutes.

An officer acquaintance once boasted that he was the replacement for the company commander. He meant that he was in charge of the few men remaining in a company that had been nearly completely wiped out. He was glad that, among his comrades, he had survived. I could not help finding his attitude reprehensible.

Of all the contagious diseases a soldier must fight, cholera is the worst. It kills in a matter of hours. Usually, a high fever and dry mouth were the first signs. Because weakness robs the body of its powers of resistance, within half an hour or so, the victim's arms and legs went numb. When things had reached this stage, there could be no doubt; it was cholera. The victim would call to friends for water. Probably the friend who brought him some would gently put a rifle by his side in case he wanted to commit suicide. By this stage, however, the sick man was usually too weak to kill himself. Saying, "Rest a few minutes; the medics'll be along in no time," the friend would hasten away. If he returned in thirty minutes, the man would already be dead.

Officers gave the command to burn the dead together with the house he died in. We gathered whatever flammable materials we

133

could find, piled them together, and lighted them. As the flames soared upward, some men screamed, "Long live the Forty-third Regiment," in voices inhumanly distorted. Others stood silently, reverently, with tears streaming down their faces. But when the fire was out, everything was over. None of us would collect the bones of the dead; we knew the fearsomeness of cholera.

Day and night the bloody battles continued. As one of the first to be repatriated, I have written only a small part of the memories that have pained me all these years. What with burnings, pillagings, and killings, the Chinese suffered more than we did. In war, both the winners and the losers must pay immense prices from which neither gains any real advantage.

Productive Use of Horror
Fumiyoshi Marubashi

IN FEBRUARY, 1931, I was sent to Shanghai, where the smoldering embers of the city told clearly of the destruction caused by the so-called Shanghai Incident of that same year. From there, I went to Manchuria, where I joined the expedition in charge of controlling that region.

In the front lines there was never enough food because the chest-deep mire covering all the roads made it impossible to ship supplies from Harbin. I remember that once we went for two months with nothing but sorghum to eat. Added to the hunger, we had to endure the cold of the mud through which we marched. Under such miserable circumstances, thoughts of home are the only thing that gives the soldier the courage to go on.

In 1937, when I was trying to cross a river under enemy fire, the truck I was driving went out of control; and I broke my arm. First I was sent to a hospital in Peking; but when the wound did

134

not heal, I was sent back to my home in Japan, where I gradually recuperated. In 1941, I received instructions to report the state of my health to the authorities. I did as I was told and by return mail received instructions to report for duty as an army worker repairing ships for the navy. This kind of thing was often necessary in those days because of the shortage of ships. I continued this job until I was discharged after the defeat.

Ordinary common sense had no meaning in military life, where orders were the sole standard. It was the soldier's duty to obey. Disobedience could lead to being shot. If an officer asked an enlisted man what he was doing, the enlisted man had to answer, "Something bad." In all likelihood he was doing nothing wrong, but this was the reply he was expected to give. It did not guarantee security from punishment, however.

Extended detail duty awaited any person who was responsible for cleanup and missed a tiny piece of dirt or fluff. Officers hit us. That was bad enough. But it was much worse when they ordered enlisted men to strike each other.

Still, this is the way military life was. There was no room for emotions, especially humane ones.

Orders in relation to the enemy were very strict and cruel. Since it was impossible for us to distinguish between the Chinese military and the ordinary civilian citizenry, in some instances we were ordered to capture everyone we found. We had to do it, whether we wanted to or not.

Once war has started, there is no way for human beings caught in it to avoid doing cruel things. It is too late to escape. This is the reason that we must attempt to ensure that wars do not occur again.

In looking back on my own military experiences, I know that I did not act on my own. Orders governed everything we did. To disobey was to be shot. The Japanese military undeniably did grave harm to the Chinese people. We cannot erase our responsibility by making mere apologies. No matter what the orders, in the final analysis, it was the individual who actually acted. Con-

135

sequently, none of us has the right to deny all blame. I think that the approach we must take is to use our experiences in a productive way, as a means toward the development of lasting peace.

Retreat to Despair
Masakatsu Nomura

I RECEIVED MY red slip of paper—draft notifications in Japan during World War II were on red paper—in August, 1943, and after training, set out for Burma. We landed at Singapore, then traveled up to Pinang, and finally crossed the Arakan mountains. I was with the ambulance corps.

The jungles were littered with corpses, many of them already half decomposed. When we stopped to eat, tigers sometimes came out of the brush. Two men were killed by them. At our assigned location, we dug trenches at the base of the hills to serve as our headquarters.

Very shortly, we fell under heavy enemy attack. The numbers of dead and injured rose steadily. Once, called out at night from a sleep, I hurried to the place where the fighting was thickest. Shells were whizzing through the darkness. Suddenly, close at hand, I heard a tremendous explosion. A mine thrower hit not far away. Bits of shrapnel flew against my back, but miraculously I was unhurt.

Farther on, a group of our troops had run into a mine field. Dead and injured lay everywhere. One corpse was still holding his blood-covered sword. Some of the men had been ripped apart. Chunks of human flesh lay scattered on the ground. Many men had lost either one or both arms or legs. We did our best to stop their bleeding before carrying them back on stretchers. But generally we were powerless to help. Blood dripped from the

136

stretchers. The men were in too much agony to cry out; they only moaned low. Most of them died soon after we arrived at camp.

Four months later we relocated to Maungdaw. The monsoon started. We slept and worked in rainwater and mud. Upon waking in the morning, we often saw elephant tracks next to our huts. Sometimes we heard the awesome roaring of tigers close by. Mosquitoes brought malaria, which took a heavy toll. New recruits lost psychological balance and suffered from something like somnambulism. I recall some soldiers who wanted tobacco so badly that they crawled into a Burmese field to steal some. The enemy spotted them and blew them to bits.

Before long, I caught malaria. First, I suffered incredible chills then a temperature of more than forty degrees centigrade. For about a week, I was on the border between life and death. But, once again miraculously, I recovered.

At about the same time, the enemy began dropping leaflets on which were printed frightening messages: "Soon it will be the dreaded mosquito season. Men bitten by these creatures lose their sexual potency; they become half-men. Come over to us. We will give you good, warm food."

Reading this, I had visions of a hot bowl of the kind of delicious bean-paste soup I had loved at home. I could only grit my teeth and try to bear it.

Raids on us became still worse. The number of casualties increased steadily. It was decided that those few of us who had survived would have to retreat down the mountains. Looking like beggars, we began wending our way through waist-deep mud toward the foothills. We had no reason to suspect that Japan had already been defeated until we found ourselves living in huts like pigsties in the Nakhon Pathom prisoner-of-war camp, in Thailand.

In the daytime, we treated the ill, then went on heavy-work details. Some people did laundry all day till their hands bled. Others were in charge of hauling drum cans full of human waste to a dumping spot eight kilometers from the camp. We labored from the dark of morning till the dark of night. A number of men became ill from exhaustion. Others were killed in landslides. During the war, the natives had especially loathed our officers. When officers became prisoners, some of them were knifed to death or beaten to death with clogs made of teak. Every day we lived in the fearsome shadow of death.

At night, I lay under a single thin blanket with my head on a wooden pillow and did my best to convince myself that I must put up with our horrible situation. But it became too desperate to tolerate. Several of us began making plans for a group escape when suddenly word was received that we were to be repatriated.

Home! Back to Japan! No words can express the happiness I felt at learning this news. The days between the arrival of the happy word and my first step on the soil of postwar Japan were long. My emotions were very mixed. I was overjoyed to be going home but unhappy at the thought of the countless other soldiers who would never make the trip.

In Japan, times were very bad. Tokushima, where I landed, had burned. Here and there people were managing to scrape together boards and pieces of steel sheet to build huts for themselves. I exchanged my military food certificates for some potato bread. It was all I could get.

I was back, and in my heart I prayed for the repose of the souls of all, friend and foe alike, who had lost their lives in the hell of war.

At Last
Hajime Kusaka

A WEEK AFTER my arrival in Manila, in May, 1943, we were sent to the north of the island to construct a base. I was with the engineers, and we had just received word that the Americans were going to land at Aparri. As it turned out, however, they actually landed at Lingayen, in the southwestern part of Luzon. From there, they moved on to capture Manila and to begin a northward march. In the line of their advance was a town called Baguio, where were located the headquarters of General Tomobumi Yamashita, the Tiger of Malaya. In order to make it possible for General Yamashita to retreat, it was necessary to build a road between the town of Baguio and another town to the north. Our organization was sent from Aparri to the Baguio region to undertake the work. The road, completed in April, 1944, made General Yamashita's retreat possible. But as the Americans' northward advance continued unabated, Japanese troops had to take up guarding positions at a pass on their way.

Our group of engineers was small. We had no bullets. Explosives were our only weapon. We installed a large quantity of them near the top of the hill at the pass and devised a hand grenade to detonate the load when the Americans approached. Gripping the hand grenade, I held my breath like a wild beast, climbed part of the way down the hill, and lay in concealment, waiting. We hoped to cause the Americans as much delay as possible.

We stayed in this position for a long time. The tension of being constantly on the lookout sharpened our animal instincts but dulled our minds and drove us nearly mad. To avoid being killed, we had to kill. The emotions of fear reached such an extreme that I could hear nothing happening around me.

A mild-mannered person who would not hurt a fly, I had been converted into an honorary killer in the name of the Japanese empire and its war. My dilemma arose from the normal human desire to live and the military man's sense of duty.

Suddenly I heard first the thundering of a tank gun from the small valley on my left, then the clattering of a caterpillar vehicle. Looking behind me, I saw the position where some of my men had been resting enveloped in dust and smoke. They had already been attacked. I was amazed by the strategy of the Americans, who had hit us while I lay foolishly watching the shots from their cannon exploding like huge peonies in the twilight.

At night, after the Americans had retreated, we found the bodies of our comrades, cruelly mangled by enemy tanks. The grove of trees where we had rested was burned black; and the rivulet, which out of nostalgia for home we had named Hirose River, was crimson with blood. A friend I had known since middle school had been directly hit. His body was blasted to bits; his sword stuck in the ground nearby, like a grave marker. By the cold glare of flares, we sat embracing the blood-bathed corpses of our friends, and wept.

Another small Japanese outfit was posted not far away. Their mission was more desperate than ours. They dug small holes beside the road to hide in. When the American tanks learned that my group had set a trap for them, they detoured from our road to the one beside which this other group lay in ambush. As the tanks approached, the Japanese soldiers, holding explosives against their chests, ran out and crawled under the treads. It was their duty. There was nothing anyone could do to help them. Like my men beside the rivulet, they all died.

We had secretly believed that dying for one's country was glorious, a joy. When we saw it in all its cruelty, we realized that death is no more than death. Patriotism has nothing to do with the issue.

Day by day, it became clearer that Japan was losing the battle of the Philippines. We were mercilessly forced to retreat toward mountain-enclosed Kiangan. The march there was one of hunger and fatigue. We had lost all dignity and wandered like a pack of wild dogs. The more we asked ourselves why we were being forced to suffer, the more doubt assailed us. Gradually we grew desperate; there was no way to resolve our doubting.

When we finally reached Kiangan, we found that there were no supplies there. To survive, we dug yams and caught crabs, rats, and snakes from the swamp. Exhausted and hungry, we were more concerned about finding something to eat than about attacking Americans.

Earlier, when our group had first landed in Aparri, the company that had been there before us was scheduled to leave. Because of a lack of trucks, they were using horse-drawn carts to transport their gear. I noticed that the wagons were loaded with all kinds of nonmilitary-looking household goods. The people of the village were walking around the carts pointing out things and identifying them as their own. The Japanese soldiers were plundering the village before departing. Lamps were especially valued, and the Japanese did not leave a single one behind. One day, a Philippine woman came to me with the complaint that a Japanese soldier had raped her. Though I did not think any of my men would do such a thing, I called them together and confronted them with the woman. But she could not find the guilty man among them. It turned out to have been someone in the recently departed company. But other similar incidents occurred during our stay.

Still, I was fortunate in my men. In those days, people were drafted into the military on the basis of four classes of physical fitness. My men were all from the lower two categories. They had barely met the qualifications for service. This meant that they moved a little slowly. But this was better because they did much less harm to the Philippine people than groups of virile young men.

In wartime, people do the most shameful things just to survive. When food runs out, a soldier will unhesitatingly steal his buddy's rice. In the struggle for something to eat, comrades were more to be feared than the enemy. The man with a small supply of rice was forced to exert all his ingenuity to protect it from theft. He would use the bag in which the rice was concealed as a pillow when he slept. Even then, there was usually a friend sitting awake beside him, waiting for him to move his head slightly. At the first chance, the vigilant thief would have the rice in his grasp.

In addition to military men, some Japanese civilians were with us during the retreat. Weaker than the soldiers, they dropped by the wayside one after another. It is hot in the Philippine Islands, and the human corpse decomposes rapidly. For a while, we were all disgusted by the odor; but soon we became so accustomed to it that we were able to eat calmly, even surrounded by the smell of death. This was less adaptation to the environment than the dehumanization of our emotions.

After arriving in Kiangan, we were at once sent to the front, where we fell under daily American attacks. Then suddenly, for no apparent reason, the American advance halted. We took the welcome relief to wash clothes and rest.

The lull continued. Finally, on September 15, 1945 — one month after the event — we received word from headquarters that Japan had surrendered. "At last!" was all we thought.

Jungles, Deadly Disease, and Madness

Tamiro Abè

WE ALL MUST HAVE HAD a premonition that the end was near. When a naval commander visited our outfit, which was stationed on Cebu, in the Philippines, two of us were ordered to be his guards on his return to headquarters. The trip should have taken about three days' walking. At the time of our departure, we were given two cups of something like cornmeal mush and a slice of the leg of a goat.

Because of the detours we were forced to make as the result of enemy attacks, our trip took five days. We ran out of food. The water we drank and the grasses we ate gave us all severe diarrhea.

142

In this condition, we arrived at headquarters, where our eyes bulged to see the abundance of food: pork and water buffalo. We devoured the water buffalo and again contracted severe diarrhea because we were unaccustomed to such food.

We had known that the area was malaria-ridden, but the information did nothing to protect us. During the first three days of our stay in a native house, we all three came down with the sickness. I had a temperature of forty-two degrees centigrade and, though covered with as many blankets as could be procured, shivered with cold. I repeated the same mumblings over and over in my state of semiconsciousness. My two companions, who could not get out of bed, became so thin that I could encircle their waists with my two hands.

The American attacks grew worse. The headquarters were forced to relocate, and the commander told us to go along. I had recovered enough to walk, but one of my comrades was still in bed. Tearfully he told me, "You go without me." But I could not abandon him. The two of us stayed behind together.

With the departure of headquarters, we lost all food supply. To dull our hunger pangs, we hunted things the natives threw away and made soup of them. Birds often lighted in the mango trees around our house. Though we sat for hours with rifles in hand, we were too weak to hit any of them. Our only hope was that before it was too late someone would come to our aid.

Over a month later, a military man turned up in front of our house. For a few moments, we stood facing each other with raised weapons. He thought we were natives, and we did not recognize him as a friend. After learning that we were Japanese soldiers, he asked us what we were doing in such a place at such a time. When we requested that he help us, he told us that the war was over. Japan had surrendered shortly after the headquarters had relocated. We had remained in ignorance for more than a month.

The soldier told us the name of the village where Japanese troops were gathering and instructed us to be there within three days. We had no food. How could we cover the distance in the allotted time? The soldier had killed a wild dog but would not share even a small bit of it with us. Nonetheless, we made it to the collecting point on time without his food or his help.

We were put into a prisoner camp to await repatriation. Philippine citizens who had lost relatives or loved ones because of the cruelty of the Japanese were instructed to tell the names of the responsible parties. If the Phillipine said, "Abè," all the Abès in the group had to form a circle while the accuser examined us and pointed out the guilty man if he were present. This process went on for so long that I was not allowed to return to Japan until 1946.

As I look back on my experiences, I see that I was at the boundary between life and death many times during World War II. For instance, the transport ship that carried me from Japan to Cebu left Sasebo, on Kyushu, on the eighth of August, 1944. At that time, the Philippine Islands were a major battle zone. American submarine attacks were so heavy that we were forced to hide in any available harbor in the day and sail only at night. We were in Manila harbor on September 20 of that same year, when the Americans first bombed the city. All the ships remaining in the port were destroyed, but ours managed to slip out to sea and safety. We learned about the danger we had been in, later.

I made it safely to Cebu, only to find that our outfit had just six months' food supply and that there would be no more, since naval shipping lanes had been cut off. Hearing that rice was available for the shock units, I weighed my life against my hunger and decided to settle for food, even at the price of great peril. It was good luck that saw me through my duty with the shock troops. Most of my comrades never returned home. Our group was not a direct combat outfit, but a radio unit. Nonetheless, the American attacks were so violent that, of thirty-five men, only three survived. Close relatives, especially mothers, and recollections about them tied us to real life. I know of not a single war comrade who died crying anything like, "Long live the emperor!"

Among the Americans, as well as among the Japanese, many military men either committed suicide or went insane. I attribute this to the inhuman scale and deadliness of the weapons used in the war and to the dread these weapons inspire. Japanese men who killed themselves on homeward-bound transport ships the minute they had a glimpse of Japan are said by some people to have died either for the glory of their country or out of a sense of shame over the surrender. I do not agree. In my eyes, their acts were the outcome of insanity.

The horror of war not only damages and destroys bodies, it deranges minds, as well. And this applies to the winners and the losers. In the collection camp after the surrender, we were housed in a building next to the American field hospital, where mad American soldiers were kept in cages. It would have been impossible to distinguish between them and apes.

Different, But Human All the Same

Tadaichi Kakitani

IN TWO DAYS, in July, 1945, both my wife and my only son died. In one week's time, I was inducted into the Japanese Engineers. Only a month later, Japan surrendered; and I was captured and sent to the town of Petrovsk on the east shore of Lake Baikal, in Siberia. As a prisoner for almost two years, I did heavy labor on engineering projects, in potato fields, and in flour mills. I even received Communist indoctrination.

In winter, temperatures dropped to minus twenty degrees centigrade. Human excrement froze at once. When anyone went outdoors and returned to the barracks, his comrades would immediately examine his nose. Without the person's knowledge, it might be so frostbitten that it could fall off his face.

Because we were given very little to eat, we sometimes stole rice in order to stay alive. Nonetheless, we all suffered from malnutrition. At one point, I weighed only thirty kilograms. When I fell ill and went to the clinic, the military doctor pinched the skin of my buttocks. I was so undernourished that the skin had lost all its elasticity and remained in a pinched-out position for a long time. I could not lie for long in one position because my bones thrust hard against my skin, causing me excruciating pain.

Not everything was horrible about my two years in the Russian prison camp. For example, I recall one old Russian woman who demonstrated the bonds of common humanity that transcend nationality when she expressed concern over my wife and children — she did not know they were dead — and her hope that I would soon be able to rejoin them.

According to the Communist system, all work has norms. A person who fulfills 100 percent of his norm is given a food bonus. I had a kind superintendent who sometimes adjusted the account in my favor. If I had fulfilled 95 percent of my norm for three days running, he would enter in the book two days under 95 percent and one day under 100 percent. His consideration for my plight made me profoundly aware of the compassion and human concern that are in all men, no matter what differences of ideology or political system may separate them.

Alone in Alien Soil
Yukiko Kamei

MY HUSBAND, who had been working in a transport company in Korea, was called into the military service in June, 1945. With no idea that Japan would lose the war, I had put my eldest son in a middle school some distance from our home in Korea only one day before all Japanese were ordered to evacuate. There were five of us. I was thirty-three at the time, and my other four children were eleven, nine, three, and less than one. Though concerned about my eldest boy away in school, I gathered together a few belongings: memorial plaques to the family ancestors, winter clothing for the children, blankets, and things for the baby. We kept our baggage to the minimum, since we had been ordered to take no more than what we could carry ourselves.

The raid we encountered on the first day out was so horrifying that some of our group went mad. Day in, day out, we continued covering an average of about twelve miles daily, mercilessly abandoning the ill and the old who could not keep up the pace. My eleven-year-old son's back was bent double under the heavy load he carried. My oldest daughter had the infant strapped to her back. It pained me to watch them struggle, but I could do nothing. I had a heavy load myself and was leading the three-year-old by the hand. We had to keep up with the group.

The people at the head of the line walked for forty-five minutes, rested for fifteen, and ordered everyone to start up again. We barely managed to stay with the pack by not resting at all.

When we came to rivers, we would wash a small amount of rice, gather twigs, make a fire, cook the rice, and eat it with a little salt or uncooked bean paste. As the evacuation march went on, we suffered menacing threats from Russian soldiers and pillage raids by Korean security troops. The children did not complain,

147

but grew thinner day by day. Soon they began having bloody bowel movements.

In the middle of September, we finally reached Hankow. The children were suffering from malnutrition and amebic dysentery. My admiration for their courage in coming this far was so great that I was unable to hold back my tears.

The city was packed with refugees to the point that walking through the streets was difficult. More than a hundred died every day from starvation and dysentery. Corpses, loaded on trucks and covered with straw mats, were hauled to the mountains for burial. Penniless, my four children and I did not know what tomorrow would bring. We were grieved to be forced to set out hungry on the road of death.

But I was soon to receive fresh hope. I found my eldest son, my twelve-year-old boy, who was as courageous and reliable as a grown man. With him, I was certain we would be able to reach home again. Embracing all my children by turns, I wept with unbounded joy.

Though the cold North Korean winter set in, we had to sell our warm clothes piece by piece for food. I felt compelled to nourish the children as best I could. When we had been at home, my breasts had amply fed the infant. Now they were dried out. All the child had eaten for two months was hot water from rice cooking and some watery cornmeal soup. Perhaps he had forgotten what food was, for he soon lost all appetite. He would open his mouth, however, whenever he saw the water bottle. He must have come to think that water was his only sustenance. He spat out anything else we put in his mouth. Whimpering softly in my arms, he grew weaker and weaker. I could not even take him to a doctor. All I could do for my child was stroke his head to keep him from disturbing the others.

In a week, he lay, a cold, mummylike corpse in my arms. Shedding scalding tears, I begged forgiveness. I, a mother, had allowed my baby to die of starvation just as he was about to be one year old.

My eldest son, one of the people in our group, and I carried my cold infant to a nearby mountain. We dug a grave and laid him, still wrapped in the padded coat in which he had lived for months, to rest in the alien ground, where he must sleep alone. As soon as the grave was filled, I longed to dig my child up again and carry him home. My oldest son, not wishing to leave his small brother, sat silent by the grave for hours.

CHAPTER FIVE

What We Have Done
Part 1

So in the sky the monstrous sun
Mocked like a punishment to be,
Extending now, to you and me
The vision of what we have done.

GEORGE BARKER
"Channel Crossing"

When man wages war today, he has armed himself to shame Jove's puny thunderbolts. The destruction of which humanity is now capable robs the sensitive of sanity. Man has given death a new power: to lurk in the flesh for years then to emerge in the hideous spots and bleeding mouths of radiation-sickness and to claim his victims at his leisure. The old gods of war must retreat, defeated, from the competition. Laughing them to scorn, man raises golden, glittering, sky-soaring mush-room clouds over infernos of crushed buildings and charred bodies. Mars himself, unable to claim omnipotence on the field of war, must shamefacedly point a finger to the new works of man, to what we have done.

Endless, Mute Parade
of the Injured
Tatsuko Mori

ON AUGUST 6, 1945, my husband left home for work at seven thirty in the morning, as usual. Shortly after his departure, my father-in-law and I left for Hesaka village to look for food, especially fresh vegetables. We left my mother-in-law at home; but on my back I carried my eldest son, who was two years old at the time. Our house was in Ushita, a wooded residential district

153

north of Hiroshima Station. We set out along the riverside road and walked north, past the barracks of the engineering battalion. Some of the men were already engaged in pontoon-building exercises and practice in digging for land mines. At the back gate of the barracks settlement, a throng of people had assembled to see off relatives recently called into military service.

As we turned into the road along the Hiroshima reservoir, I pointed to a cluster of planes in the distance. My father-in-law and I agreed that they were B-29s. But why were they there? The all-clear had sounded before we left home.

Suddenly, we were enveloped in what seemed to be a huge magnesium flare. Then we were overcome with a dull heat wave. Instinctively I took cover in a narrow space between two buildings. My child was still on my back, and my father-in-law fell on top of us. Several other people crowded into the same space.

Immediately following the flash there was a tremendous explosion. A mighty air wave seemed to lift me upward. In the next moment, I was being crushed against the ground by ponderous pressure. The force of the explosion raised a cloud of swirling black dust mixed with wood fragments and slivers of broken glass. All of us were injured or cut.

Following the first shock, the others in our small space scattered in all directions. The neighborhood in which we had been walking only minutes ago was chaos. Thick dust obscured my view at first, but it gradually settled, revealing fires shooting skyward all over the city. The Ushita district was demolished. The streets were a clutter of fallen telephone poles and tangled wires. Fires, living demons lashed to fury by the gusts of winds from the blast, spread with terrifying rapidity and belched billows of black smoke. We were nearly out of our wits with fear.

Groups of refugees fled hither and thither in confusion. But my father-in-law and I headed directly for my parents' temporary home in Hesaka. My son's legs and hands had been burned and were swelling. Before going to my parents, we stopped at the office of the village doctor. But he had been called to the local

154

elementary school, which had been designated as an evacuation center.

The school courtyard was already crowded with wounded victims of the bombing. Still others continued to stream in. How could these battered people have made it this far in their frightful condition? They were all cut, burned, and bleeding. Peeled skin revealed raw flesh. Hair was burned and frizzled. Vacant eyes stared from scorched, blackened faces. The people were in too much pain to be hungry, but they all craved water. They got none, however, because it was believed that even a mouthful would kill people in such a condition as theirs. The sights I was witnessing intensified my hatred of war. Many of the people who had fled to the school for help were beyond first-aid measures. They died one after the other.

No one knew how to treat the unusual injuries of the wounded because we were all shocked and stunned, and ignorant of the nature of this sudden and inexplicable catastrophe. After a while I left for my parents' house without obtaining medical attention for my son. The wait would have been too long, and I was at the point of nausea and fainting from the nightmare I had witnessed.

At my parents' house, both my father-in-law and I were desperate with worry over my mother-in-law, left at home. We had to do something to try to help her. We decided that it might be faster and safer to go back to Ushita through the mountains. I wrapped my son's head in a cloth, strapped him to my back, and joined my father-in-law on the road. Neighbors gave us directions.

We climbed the mountain but, on reaching the top, encountered groups of half-naked, wounded refugees fleeing from the Ushita district, which, they said, was engulfed in flames as far as the foot of the mountain. Frightened and worried, we made up our minds to go back to my parents; but in our distress, we lost our way and wandered into a dense chestnut forest that we had not passed on the way up.

Sharp-edged grasses cut our feet and legs as we plunged through underbrush. In places, the land fell away so sharply that we had to tie my father-in-law's belt around tree trunks and lower ourselves by means of it. The heat of midsummer fatigued us and made us thirsty. Part of the way down the slope, we came on a track leading to a cottage. We approached and asked the owner for water. He drew some from the well, but it was too muddy to drink. The water from that well was usually clear, he told us. He kindly showed us the way we should follow and finally we found my parents' house, where we enjoyed long drinks of delicious, cold well water.

Still, we could not resign ourselves to abandoning my mother-in-law in the sea of flames of Ushita. This time we decided to try to reach our house by way of the river road. We went out and started on our way, only to find the road packed with refugees with horse-drawn carts, handcarts, tricycles, bicycles, and any vehicle that promised hope of escape, as well as a great throng of pedestrians. The apparently endless stream pushed steadily in the direction opposite to the one in which we wanted to travel. It was hopeless: we could not battle such a flood.

All of them were burned or injured. Stricken with anxiety and fear, they walked on helplessly, aimlessly pushed by the great surge behind them. Some exhausted people fell by the wayside but no one thought of coming to their aid. Those with the remaining strength plodded on, mute and thoughtless. The wind carried their pungent, infernal stench up the river.

Defeated again, with a prayer that my mother-in-law was safe, we returned to my parents' house. Shortly after our arrival, we were overjoyed to see my elder brother and my mother-in-law. Though he was seriously wounded in the forehead and in both hands, she was completely unharmed. She had been in the kitchen when the bomb exploded. The roof had collapsed, pinning her under it. But she had managed to extricate herself and had waited for some member of the family to find her.

We resolved to spend the night with my parents. We were all present except my husband. Naturally, I was frantic with worry about him and prayed for his safety.

156

Before going to bed, I went to the bathroom and saw my face in a mirror for the first time that day; it was burned a dark tan and ached as if it had been pricked deeply with something sharp. I took off my blouse. It had been white when I put it on that morning. It was gray. I dipped it in water to wash it. The blouse disintegrated as if it were made of tissue paper.

The terrifying events of the day kept me awake through the interminable night. Early the next morning, I got out of bed and went outside. In the predawn light, I saw wounded refugees lying on the ground. They had come as far as their strength would take them and had collapsed. Looking at them, I seemed to hear echoes of the distant groans of the dying in the city. The forms of the trees in the garden were beginning to detach themselves from the gloom of night. They sparkled with fresh, morning dew. But the horrors were about to begin again.

Flame and Black Rain

Satoko Matsumoto

FOR SEVERAL DAYS the weather had been hot and clear. We were hoping against hope for a little cooling rain. The previous night, the air-raid alarm had sounded several times. I was sweaty with having run back and forth between the house and the shelter and wanted to take a bath. With a bar of the poor-quality soap that was regarded as a treasure in those days, I washed my body and started washing my hair. Soap suds got in my eyes. I was blinking helplessly when a tremendous flash of light suddenly swept over everything. Throwing on some clothes, I picked up my two-year-old daughter, who was playing under a chair in the living room. It was lucky that she was indoors. Often, in summer, she went out to play in nothing but panties.

Suddenly, as I was holding her to me, the house collapsed, pinning us under the wreckage. My first efforts to extricate myself and my daughter only brought more debris tumbling down on us. Slowly and carefully, I crawled out. It took a long time. Once out of doors, I was appalled at what I saw. Every building in the city seemed to have been razed. Nothing stood to give any indication of the familiar skyline that had been there only minutes earlier. Mount Eba, never visible from our house, stood clearly revealed in front of me.

In the swirling dust and smoke, I could make out ghostly human figures moving toward us from the east. The roads were buried under rubble, and the people picked their way among ruins. Some of them were completely naked. Others had on trousers. Only a few carried bundles. At first, I thought I noticed tatters of clothing hanging from some of them. Then I realized that it was skin flayed from their bodies to expose raw flesh. A woman — it was at first hard for me to determine her sex — was wandering about, oblivious of her own condition but calling the names of her loved ones. When my own husband had died some time earlier, I had thought I knew the meaning of hell; but what I had experienced then could not be compared with what confronted us all in the destroyed and burning city.

Fire had started spreading from all directions. Not one of the fire wardens, who usually strutted about with such self-importance, was to be seen. I heard someone shout that we must hurry if we wanted to cross the river, for the Oguchi Bridge had caught fire. I immediately decided to cross and to head for the foot of the mountain in the western part of the city, which seemed to be the only safe place. A man who had been walking in front of me fell to the ground. Putting out my hand to help him, I saw that he was already dead. One after another, people died, some of them with a cry for water on their lips.

Then it began to rain, large, heavy drops lashing the wounded flesh of the burned. In agony, these people fled to nearby fields to hide under whatever vegetation they could find. Before long, I

158

noticed something strange about the rain. It was not clear and fresh, but dark, turbid, and sticky, like crude oil. It adhered to my hair and to my skin, which were already covered with reddish dust from the debris of my collapsed house.

As the rain began to let up, American aircraft flew in from the south, circled low, and flew northward. Some of the refugees from the Hiroshima holocaust shook their fists at them and cursed. By the time we reached the foothills, the number of refugees had diminished. I at first entertained the idea of crossing a small river not far away and going to the other side of the mountain to a village to which I had sent some of my personal property for safekeeping. Then I remembered what I had been told at the time. The people there were willing to accept luggage for storage but did not welcome refugees. There was already a food shortage in their village, and extra mouths to feed could not be tolerated. After reflecting for a while, I saw that the only thing for me to do was to return to what was left of our home in the hope of finding some food. On our way back we saw countless corpses charred and spattered with blackish rain. In a shallow river dead bodies lay in twisted, grotesque positions. I could only hope that the tide would come and wash them out to sea.

Back at the place where our house had once stood, I began to rummage among the rubble to find food, and especially one emergency sack — bearing a tag with our name on it — in which I had set aside a small store of provisions. It had apparently been stolen. I wanted to wash our clothing, but there was no water. In the evening, by the light of the raging fires, I was continuing the search for food when I found the small child of one of our neighbors. The little girl, who was pinned under the wreckage of a house, was smeared with dust, excrement, and dried urine. I could not imagine what might have prompted the mother, usually completely devoted to her daughter, to abandon her this way.

Throughout the long night, with the two babies at my side, I sat clutching my widow's pension certificate, my only hope for an income, and resolved not to let the ordeal of the days ahead

159

defeat me. Earlier, both my mother-in-law and my own elder brother had left Hiroshima without telling me. At the time, I had felt alone and betrayed. Now I held no grudge. I was glad that they had evacuated the city before the great havoc descended.

I had suffered no external injury; still it was painful to spend the interminable night on the damp ground in the lurid glow of the fire that was consuming what was left of the city. Occasionally, black shadows of American aircraft passed overhead. I saw many shooting stars flash across the sky. Someone sent a chill up my spine by saying that the unusual number of them must mean that many soldiers were dying in the islands of the South Pacific.

In the gloom of the night, I found no rest. At first, I moved to try to find a spot not soaked with dew. In my new position, I heard people calling for water. There was none to give them, and I could not bear listening to the agonized pleas. I moved again, this time to find myself next to a person praying to the Amida Buddha over the body of a dead man. Once again, I moved. I spent the entire night wandering from one place to another.

In the morning, someone brought a supply of balls of steamed rice for us, but the heat of the summer and of the fires had caused the rice to sour. As hungry as we were, we found it difficult to eat the spoiled food. The heat had other grim effects. It caused wounds to fester and to breed maggots. Flies tormented the victims by clustering on their open wounds.

As the sun rose higher in the sky, the heat became intolerable. Finally, I found an old shutter door that I used to make a shade under which we could rest. From a broken pipe nearby a thin trickle of water dripped. We washed our faces and hands with it but were unable to remove the stains left by the black rain of the day before. All around us, people — even those who were apparently healthy — continued to fall down dead.

Later the same day, I returned to our neighborhood, where I learned that a village called Miyauchi had been designated as our evacuation location. With the two babies, I set out at once. It took us a whole day to reach the village, where we were allowed to

160

remain only three days before being forced to return to Hiroshima.

Gradually I grew lonely for my own family. On August 14, 1945, the three of us set out for the village of Kuchi, my mother's home village. I did not know what would await us there. I suspected that the house where my mother had been born and raised would be too small to accommodate us. Still, I wanted to go where there were people I might know.

When we arrived in Kuchi, I found to my relief that my mother, father, and younger brother and younger sister had escaped the horror of Hiroshima and were living in the house of our uncle, a poor farmer. My daughter and I were afflicted with diarrhea and we had lice. When I remember them, even today, my head itches. The day after we reached Kuchi, the war ended.

My father was injured, though apparently not seriously. Before long, however, he developed symptoms of radiation sickness, notably petechia, or purple spots on the skin. He suffered great pain. On the evening of August 22, when he had gone to the field to try to take his mind off his agony, he suddenly fell dead.

Intolerable Recollections
Izumi Izuhiro

IT MIGHT HAVE occurred yesterday, the memory is so vivid. Whenever I recall what happened after the bombing of Hiroshima, I cannot restrain my tears.

My husband, who had been drafted into military service, was working at an army division headquarters in the city. On the morning of August 6, 1945, our daughter, Takako, then a freshman in a girls' school, left home in high spirits. She said, "We must keep up our courage and strength until we win the war."

161

I went into the bathroom to draw a bath. I knew that Takako would be home at noon, and I thought a bath would refresh her. While there, I heard some schoolchildren shouting, "Look! A parachute!" I looked out the window and saw the parachute descending slowly. Something was dangling from it.

In the next instant, a blinding blue flash struck. I was hurled to the floor. A giant mushroom-shaped cloud rose into the sky. It did not fade. The blast blew the roof off the house, smashed all the windows, and destroyed almost everything inside. Before much longer, a black rain fell and drenched all the tatami mats on the floors.

Outside I saw people dragging what at first looked like white cloth but what I later saw was skin that had peeled from their bodies. Some of them came into the remains of our house. They lay down on the wooden floor of the veranda and begged for water or for some kind of covering. Many of them were extremely cold, though the weather was blazing hot. I could do so little to help them. When I gave some water to a schoolgirl who had been blinded and whose hair was singed and crinkly, she thanked me, said she would never forget my kindness, and died in agony.

In my concern for my own children and my husband, I made two trips to a nearby bridge that they had to cross to come home. But the city was ablaze, and I could not travel farther alone. All along the roadside lay people dead or dying and calling for water, for help, for their mothers. Nearby a school was still standing. It was being used as an emergency center. I helped carry some people from the wreckage of their homes to the school.

In the evening, my husband returned. He was pale but had managed to walk home, barefoot, from Futaba, where he had taken refuge. Sitting on the front stone steps, he asked for water. When he had drunk some, he said he had eaten nothing since breakfast. I gave him a ball of steamed rice, but he tasted only a little before he was forced to lie down.

Soon an acquaintance came to tell us he knew where our

162

daughter was. He said she was in need of help. Half dead himself, my husband nevertheless rose; and the two of us set out to find her. We took a stretcher. My husband leaned on me all the way. We left at eight in the evening; but because we had to walk over dead bodies and needed to rest every ten meters because of my husband's condition, it was midnight when we reached the site of the prefectural government office, where our daughter was said to be. My husband called her name several times. "Here I am," a voice cried. But when we reached the place from which the sound came, I could not believe it was my daughter. She was blind, and her back had been burned bright red. She had been lying in a sea of flames. Nearby we found a cart to carry her in. We reached the remains of our house at about five in the morning. My husband had been forced to lean on the cart as we crept along.

We told Takako she was home. She thanked us both. Knowing she liked tomatoes, I gave her some slices of one that I discovered in the kitchen. She seemed to be enjoying them while she ate. But then she complained of pain. As I lifted her head on my lap, with a short groan, she breathed her last.

At about eight in the morning, our son, a student in middle school, returned. His face was pale, and his shirt was stained with blood. At the sight of his disfigured sister and at word that she was now dead, he wept from grief and shock.

Before long, all my husband's hair fell out. His face turned ashen pale. He bled from the nose, the mouth, and the anus and ran a high temperature. I tried to cool his forehead with well water. Muttering, "I've never felt such pain before. Everything in me must be ruptured," he died in an agony I could hardly bear to witness.

Courage of Desperation

Kazuo Matsumuro

THE ALL-CLEAR was sounded at seven thirty that morning. In those days, to minimize the emotional upset of its effect on the people, it was given by means of megaphones instead of loudspeakers. Probably like all the other citizens of Hiroshima, I thought the alarm had been given because of reconnaissance planes, which flew over daily.

I do not know how many minutes lapsed; but when I came to, I was imprisoned in a dark, cramped, dusty place. No matter how hard I tried, I could not move. I was nauseated. Where was I? What had happened?

In the next minute, I became aware of the crackling sound of flames. "The house is on fire!" I knew only one thing: I was alive and had to save myself somehow. As the faces of my wife, children, and parents flashed through my mind, I tried to call out. I doubt that I made a sound. I was obsessed with the desire to go on living; and I heard desperate cries from outside, from other people who did not want to die.

Something huge — a great beam — lay on my chest. I tried to move it. It would not budge. With a desperate effort, I managed to free my left arm. Encouraged, I continued to strive to break free. My head struck something, and I saw a shaft of light. The beam was starting to give way. Clawing and struggling frantically, I liberated myself from its weight.

Crawling out, I saw that my house was no more than a heap of broken timbers, smashed tiles, shattered glass. I was sick at my stomach and weak. Blood gushed from gaping wounds in my thighs. I was bleeding from my ears, nose, and mouth. But to my relief, there seemed to be nothing wrong with my abdomen.

Heat from the flames raging everywhere forced me to cover my face with my hands. Struggling to my feet, I felt a stabbing

164

pain in the waist. Later I learned that I had fractures in the bones of my back and hips.

By a miracle, I found my eyeglasses — unbroken — and put them on. Swirling smoke and dust clouds obliterated almost all light. Here and there, thin shafts of sunlight broke through. And sparks showered from rapidly spreading fires. Laboriously I walked toward what had been the street but was now a tangle of fallen timbers and telephone wires.

Picking my way through the debris, I heard an urgent cry for help. I looked in the direction of the sound, where, under the wreckage of a fallen two-story building, I saw a young mother and her small daughter pinned between a broken rafter and a cabinet of some kind. Though they could move a little, they could not get out. Thrusting out a hand, the mother screamed for help. Part of the wreckage of the house was already in flames. But I heard many other calls for help, some already weak and resigned from people soon to be swallowed in a great maw of fire.

Occasionally half-naked, blood-covered men emerged from the wall of flames. Like ghosts, they scurried about in search of safety. Some of them had been exposed to powerful radiation. As they outstretched their limp hands, the skin peeled off and hung from their fingernails. Blood oozed from raw flesh exposed by monstrous burns. None of them made a sound. They were too stunned to weep or cry out.

Gradually, the dust settled, and the smoke thinned. The only blot on the blue, clear, midsummer sky was a gigantic mushroom-shaped cloud glittering golden as it spiraled upward.

Staggering to a nearby river, I observed refugees wandering about, apparently too dazed to mind the broiling heat of the fires. On the river bank, a woman stooped over a severely injured man and shaded his face from the sun with a hat. She was praying. Hair remained on the front part of the man's skull. It had been burned away entirely from the back.

Walking as best I could to the Tsurumi Bridge, I noticed that the sea tide had raised the water level. Refugees swarmed at the shore. I thought some of them were swimming, but I immediately realized they were floating and dead. On the stone steps leading into the water sat a man in his early fifties, half in the water, half out. Then, dead, he rolled into the river and floated slowly away.

On the other side of the bridge, I saw a pretty little girl of about five lying on her back in the middle of the road. Wearing nothing but panties, she was holding her burned arms high to keep them from coming into contact with the many slivers of glass buried in her chest. The midsummer heat beat down on her mercilessly. "Please give me some water." She had probably pleaded this way with other passersby: she spoke automatically and unconsciously. The sight of her broke my heart. My own daughter, from whom I was now separated, was the same age.

"The soldiers will come soon and give you medicine and water. If you drink now, it will only make you hurt more. Be a good girl and wait a little longer."

I moved on to what seemed to be a safe place in a back alley leading eastward toward Mount Hiji. Later, I came back to see how the little girl was. She had already died.

During the sleepless night I spent on Mount Hiji, I made up my mind to look for my parents, who had been in the Yaga district of the city. I would have to go to Hiroshima Station first and then follow the tracks to Yaga. Though I was in no condition to walk long distances, I had to do what I could to find them and rescue them — if they were still alive.

Limping, almost crawling, I reached Tsurumi Bridge, where, owing to the action of the current, the river was nearly at a standstill. People in clean clothing — obviously from neighboring towns — were observing a riverboat engaged in some kind of operation. Soldiers on the boat were trying to accomplish the difficult and grisly task of disposing of corpses. There were too many to lift to the deck. The soldiers tied the bodies together with rope and tugged them as they would have pulled a raft. Even after the operation was repeated many times, there were still more corpses floating on the river.

Crossing the bridge, I passed the place where, on the day before, I had heard the call of the imprisoned mother. The house had burned. Scattered about were charred, crisp human bodies. There must have been more in the debris.

Near the place where the Koi Hospital had stood, an old woman was busily chipping at a burned telephone pole with a rock the size of her fist. On the ground nearby lay the dead body of a boy of four or five. The old woman was collecting chips and slivers of wood from the pole and sprinkling them on the body of her grandson, whom she hoped to cremate. Patiently, stoically, silently, she continued her labor with mechanical motions. She shed no tears; and in spite of my profound sympathy for her, I could shed none.

The many refugees thronging the streets all outstripped me, since I could walk only very slowly. Swarms of maggots — alive in spite of the death-dealing radiation of the bomb — feasted on flesh of the human beings in whose bodies they had hatched. My worry about my parents intensified. I was impatient with myself for being too injured to move faster. In my heart, I prayed for them and said, "Take courage. Live. I'll come. I'll rescue you, even if I must crawl all the way. Wait!"

Normally, it is possible to walk from Mount Hiji to Hiroshima Station in twenty minutes. Smeared with blood, sweat, and dust, I needed four hours to cover the distance.

Miraculous Survival

Eiichi Sakogoshi

IN AUGUST, 1945, I was a medical corpsman at the First Army Hospital, at Motomachi, Hiroshima. Our hospital was considered the finest of its kind in all Japan. In addition to my corpsman duties, I was an orderly for the hospital general affairs section, I prepared lunch for the officers and, in the afternoon, delivered papers and documents to military units located throughout Hiroshima. I liked my afternoon work best because I was usually finished early enough to stop at our house for a snack and a chat with my mother.

On August 5, 1945, as usual, I made my rounds and dropped in at our house. It was getting dark, and no one was there. Our next-door neighbor told me that mother had gone to the public bath. I went into the kitchen and ate something. Then, before returning to my outfit, I asked the same neighbor to tell mother I had been by and that I had eaten some food I found in the kitchen. I did not know then that I had missed my last chance to see my mother.

Shortly after I returned to our unit, B-29s began circling overhead. They flew about all night. None of us slept because we had to make shelter provisions in the event of a raid. At dawn, we ate breakfast and went to the hospital field, where daily morning assemblies were held. August 6 was a fine, hot summer day.

After assembly, I returned to the office, where I heard the radio announcement that the air-raid alarm in effect earlier in the morning had been lifted. The radio began to buzz with static when suddenly a great flash of yellow light swept over the earth. "A direct hit on us," I thought. It lasted only a moment, but it seemed very long to me.

Lying on the floor, I knew I was injured and thought I might be dying. The faces of my mother and others close to me flashed through my mind. Then I was suddenly awake. Crawling from under the rubble, I looked around and was appalled to see that the city had disappeared. I could see for miles, all the way to Ujina, the southern tip of Hiroshima. The much-vaunted First Army Hospital was a heap of wreckage. Hiroshima Castle — gone.

Then I glanced at myself and realized that like the city I was disfigured beyond recognition. The skin had peeled from my face. My head was bleeding and burned. Strange objects seemed

168

to be lodged in it. Then I felt an excruciating pain in my back. My shirt was on fire. Rolling in the dirt, I put out the flames. Checking to make certain that none of my other garments was burning, I immediately began to look for a place to hide in safety.

The hospital was infernal chaos. Scores of bodies littered the ground. Pandemonium reigned in the demolished hospital, where soldiers, nurses, and other people on duty were now reduced to the same wretched condition as the patients. Some scurried about aimlessly; others fell to the ground to wait for death. For the first time, I was brought face to face with the horrifying reality of war, and I was overcome with fear.

All of us soldiers had been prepared to die, but I had always hoped that with luck I would survive the war to return to ordinary civilian life. But now, with death striking all around with ghastly speed, the possibility of my living seemed remote. Terror gripped me.

I ran desperately as far as the Aioi Bridge over the Ota River. The heat from the fires raging around me and the pain of my wounds became intolerable. I jumped into the shallow river and stood, water to my shoulders, as my pain subsided little by little. Of the many other people who fled into the cooling waters, not one was completely uninjured. One of the refugees, who turned out to be an army surgeon, stood near me. I told him about my injuries and asked what I could do to help myself. For a long time, he stood silent, then with an air of stupefied resignation said, "None of us can do anything. They've dropped something awful. What can it be?"

Burning buildings collapsing into the river had heated the water. Everything seemed to be aflame. I climbed on the bank and began to run along the river's edge. I had to get away. I would suffocate from the heat if I remained there.

Finally, as I approached the mountains, I began to be able to breathe freely. A cool, fresh wind caressed my burned body and face. "Real air, at last," I thought, luxuriating momentarily in the scent of the breeze. But at that very moment, I collapsed to the ground and vomited a yellowish liquid. Nausea was followed by a horrible thirst. My throat seemed to be on fire. Struggling to my feet, I rushed in search of water. Apparently alone in the area, I found a broken pipe in the wreckage of a house and drank deep of the water flowing from it. But no matter how much I drank, in a matter of two or three minutes, the scorching thirst returned.

As I walked northward in search of more water, the sun turned deep red, as if it had been thickly painted with blood. Twilight, then darkness descended. It began raining great greasy, blackish drops of a substance that did not seem to be water. I felt as if the end of the earth had come.

Just when my thirst had become unbearable again, I came upon some men from the Kure Naval Base distributing water to victims of the bomb. I joined the group, crying, "Water, water!" But the seamen would allow us to have only a little at a time, since too much would be bad for our burns. What they gave was not enough for me. I retraced my steps in the hope of finding the broken pipe again. But I could not.

I became aware of a throbbing pain in my head, which made a strange sound at each step I took. I felt as if something heavy, something liquid, were lodged in my skull. When I shook my head, blood gushed, covering almost my entire body. With exploratory fingers, I touched the top of my head and found splinters of glass embedded in my flesh.

But I had to go on. I was raised in this part of the country and knew that there were streams in the mountains. Climbing one hill in the Ushita district, I located a small stream, just as I had suspected I would. First, I drank the fresh, cool water, then bathed my body. There was no one else around. Sitting in the clear mountain stream, I looked up at the sky and began to think of many things.

I longed for the war to end, for the army to be disbanded. But what was going to happen to us, to Japan? What of the people who managed to survive the Hiroshima bombing. I thought of my mother. I knew she could not have survived. I had seen the whole

170

neighborhood of our house in raging flames. But, unable to weep, I slept.

In a few hours I woke. It was completely dark, but the city was still aflame. Descending the mountain, I found an improvised first-aid station where hundreds of refugees were receiving treatment. I too was treated. Someone gave me a cigarette to smoke, and I returned to the mountain, where I spent the rest of the night.

For the next two weeks, I roamed aimlessly about the district where our house had stood. I no longer remember clearly what I did during that period; but I know that though I had given her up for dead I continued to search for my mother. It was some time before I learned for certain that she had been killed when the bomb exploded.

Later I was hospitalized in the Hiroshima Red Cross Hospital. For two or three months, I hovered between life and death. Even after I was released from the hospital I had to return periodically for treatment. Somehow, I pulled through the worst, but I was under treatment until the end of the year. Then I was evacuated to a place called Muro, a village facing the Seto Inland Sea. I walked there on crutches; it took three days.

Having come from a devastated city, I found the sea and mountains both beautiful and soothing. From this point began my struggle with the symptoms of radiation sickness. They persisted for years, and it is miraculous that I have survived at all.

Earthly Hell
Chizuko Kijima

IN AUGUST, 1945, I was living in the Ujina district of Hiroshima with my husband and our second son, who was two at the time. I was six months pregnant. In accordance with the government policy to evacuate as many invalids, expectant mothers, infants, and schoolchildren as possible, we had sent our elder boy to the country when his kindergarten had been closed. For a number of reasons, in spite of my pregnancy, it was impossible for me to go with him.

Until that time, Hiroshima had been spared the intensive bombing raids that other major Japanese cities had suffered. But because of the numerous strategic industries, shipyards, and military installations in the city, we were constantly in fear that our turn would come soon. Ujina would be an especially important target because in it were located a provisions depot and barracks for the Akatsuki Corps, the army equivalent of the navy Kamikaze.

In those days, all of us underwent mandatory military training. My husband, a dentist, had to attend daily training as a military doctor for a period of time. (Fortunately, he completed the course on August 5, 1945, and was not at the center when the bomb fell. Most of the people there were killed.) Though pregnant, I too was forced to take part in razing potentially dangerous buildings and in classes in the use of bamboo spears, which we were supposed to use in the event of the final, decisive battle on the home islands. Our training was held at a Shinto shrine in Ujina. We stood at attention and awaited commands from noncommissioned officers. But for me, there was no meaning in the whole undertaking. Whenever an air-raid signal sounded, with one child strapped to my back and another in my womb, I was always the last to be able to take cover. If we should have to fight on the home islands, I would be unable to make use of the bamboo spears.

One day, American aircraft dropped leaflets over Hiroshima. I saw none of them myself, but I was told that they contained a warning to the innocent citizens to evacuate the city. The Americans said they did not want civilian casualties. The military police issued orders forbidding us to read the leaflets and commanding us to pick them up and turn them in to the authorities. "They are nothing but a trick on the part of the devilish Americans and savage British," they told us. The order forbidding us to read the leaflets was senseless. Because we trusted completely in the invincibility of Japan, we probably would not have believed them even if we had read them. Still, we were frightened because we knew that only recently the Americans had mounted a massive air raid on the neighboring city of Kure, where countless civilians had perished.

August 6, 1945, was hot and clear, as had been August 5. Shortly after breakfast, when the air-raid alarm sounded, I dashed to put on the pantaloons and quilted jacket that we always wore at such times. But just as I was about to take my son and leave for the shelter, the all-clear sounded. I took off the pantaloons and jacket and was opening the closet for fresh clothes when there was an unearthly flash of light and a tremendous roar. The next moment, I was blown down by a concussive wave. Then everything went dark.

Grabbing my son, I jumped into the earthen-floored entrance way of the house. I started to run for the shelter but stopped at the threshold. Outside, the ground was covered with shattered tiles and splintered glass. I was barefoot. I quickly changed my mind and, pushing my son under the floor boards, crawled in after him. In the courtyard, I heard the shouts of my husband. He seemed to be running toward the shelter.

When the dust settled and I could see better, I put on some shoes and went outside. My husband had come back. His face, like those of all the neighbors I saw, was burnt black. Our house was a skeleton. The roof and posts and beams remained, but all the walls and everything inside except a litter of debris were gone. Even the doorsills had been blown away.

My husband washed his face, took his first-aid kit, and left for the medical station. I followed him to the road, where I saw streams of injured people heading in the same direction. Many of them were bleeding. I had suffered no external injuries, but my mind was so dazed that I cannot recall having a feeling of being spared anything.

173

When night came, it was pitch dark because there was no electricity. I went into our neighborhood to see what was happening and found people bundling up blankets and other bedding to go to spend the night on the beach. I could not follow them. I lacked the strength to carry bedding that far. Besides, I could not leave my husband, who was caring for the injured at the medical station.

Strapping my child on my back, I walked to the station. On the way, I saw Hiroshima, a sea of flames pouring vast billows of smoke into the night sky. The medical center was an inferno of heat, sickness, and death. The raw flesh of monstrously disfigured human beings gaped from open wounds. My husband was allowing the thirsty to drink, mouthful by mouthful, slowly, from the spout of a brass kettle. His padded, civilian-service uniform was drenched with sweat. He had eaten nothing since morning and was too busy even to talk with me. I went outside and waited all night for him to finish. During that night, countless people died in agony. My husband returned home for a brief while in the morning and then went back to the medical center that day and the next, and the next, and for I do not remember how many more days.

Sometime during this period, we were joined in our skeleton house—which was adequate shelter, since the weather was hot—by Dr. and Mrs. Fukuchi. Dr. Fukuchi, who ran a dental clinic, had been evacuated for a time to the country but had returned. His house and offices were completely destroyed in the blast, and the two of them were in need of a place to stay. We made do, though, throughout the several days they were with us, we had hardly anything that could be dignified by the name food.

On August 11, I went to the medical center at Ujina Port to look for my brother-in-law. He had been crushed by the collapsed rear gate of Hiroshima Castle, which housed divisional headquarters during the war and where he had been on guard at the time of the bombing. Bending down to look into the charred, deformed faces of hundreds of soldiers writhing in excruciating

174

pain in the spacious oblong earthen-floored hall of the center, I tried to identify my brother-in-law among the inhabitants of what can only be described as an earthly hell. Finally, I recognized him and, after lengthy, complicated negotiations, took him home. But he was with us only until the morning of August 16, when, with a heart-rending cry, he died. Army headquarters people took his body away and cremated it with many others. We knew the bones they gave us as his remains were anonymous.

Toward the end of 1945, I gave birth to a little girl who lived only a year. For some time, my second son suffered from diarrhea that caused bloody fluxes a dozen times a day. There was no medicine and there were few doctors in Hiroshima then. Giving up hope, one grim day, my husband advised me to prepare myself for the boy's death. I held his emaciated body in my arms. I had no tears.

But miraculously he did not die. Later Dr. Fukuchi gave us some medicine that he had received while in the country. Thanks to this medicine, my son escaped death.

The Illness That Followed
Mitsuko Hatano

ONE OF MY elder brothers was killed in action during World War II. Shortly after his death, my father fell ill; and I left Hiroshima, where I had been working with an elder sister, and returned home to care for him. At first, I worked at the Yokogawa Station of the Sanyo Main Line of the National Railways; but later I transferred to the Ibaraichi Station on the Geibi Line, which was closer to our home.

On August 6, 1945, I reported to work at the customary time. As one of the other station workers and I sat talking, we suddenly

175

heard an eerie, infernal roaring sound. The stationmaster and some of the others began shouting.

"Incendiary bombs on Kabe!"

"Look at that cloud."

Rushing to the window, I saw a gigantic cloud mushrooming upward into the sky. One of the workers who had been cleaning the station yard called, "I saw a flash of light just before the explosion."

"But it's not Kabe. It must have been Yokogawa Station."

"No. Much closer. Maybe it was Yaga."

The freight train from Hiroshima, due at our station at nine in the morning, pulled in several hours late. The engineer, grotesquely burned and bleeding, gasped, "Hiroshima! Wiped out completely!"

He was the first victim we saw, but the passenger train that arrived next brought more. Most of them were people I should have recognized. They were daily commuters between our station and Hiroshima. But they were so burned, so disfigured, and in such anguish that they scarcely seemed human. Their charred and blackened faces were all anonymous. Peeled skin hung in strips from their bodies. Many of them were unable to walk to the ticket gate. While a relative was saying, "You're at home at last; you're back now," one gravely injured man nodded and died. Much has been written about Hiroshima, but no words can describe the horrors and suffering we witnessed on that day and on succeeding days.

My elder sister had remained working in Hiroshima when I returned to live in our family home. My mother and father and I were frantic with worry about her. But all lines of communication were severed. We could do nothing but wait. Still, days passed without word. Finally, I decided to go to Hiroshima to look for her. My bedridden father could not go with me, but a neighbor, who was searching for someone herself, offered to accompany me.

Both of us were familiar with Hiroshima as it had been, but we were unprepared for the total desolation we encountered. None of the familiar landmarks were standing. The only identifiable feature was the Inland Sea in the distance. We wandered aimlessly, unable to know where we were or where we ought to go, until hunger and the blazing summer sun overcame us.

Over thirty years have passed; but I am still haunted by the city of debris, mounds of corpses, and skeletal remains of buildings. Near a place called Tsurumi, I saw a half-naked, mangled mother drinking water from a broken pipe. Her face was nearly destroyed, but her infant suckled her breast, from which the skin hung in tatters.

I searched everywhere for my sister. I went to the place where her apartment had stood and to the location where her office had once been. It was in the neighborhood of what is today called the Atomic-bomb Dome, that is, at the hypocenter of the explosion. A layer of white ash covered the ruins that were all that remained. Soldiers were attempting to haul away the corpses buried in heaps of broken tiles, shattered glass, and charred wood. But the dead were too numerous for the living to attend to.

Days of searching produced no signs of my sister. Since it seemed improbable that she could have survived, I collected a few still-warm bones from the ground, wrapped them in cloth, and took them home to my waiting parents. For days, I had walked over ground where it was said grass would not grow for seventy years.

For a long time, I suffered no ill effects. In 1948, I married. I gave birth to three children and remained in apparently good health. Then, after the birth of my fourth child, I began to suffer from a strange, inexplicable illness. I became weak and debilitated and grew steadily thinner until I weighed only half my normal weight. I consulted a doctor, who told me that he would not answer for my life unless I was hospitalized at once. I did as he suggested and got better. But ever since then, the symptoms of this illness that followed Hiroshima have periodically recurred.

I have recounted my experiences here and I often discuss the matter with my children in the hope that knowledge of our suf-

177

ferings can inspire the younger generations with a determination to abolish nuclear weapons and warfare.

The Duty of the Survivors
Sumiko Kirihara

AS IS CUSTOMARY in Japan, at the death of my father, our family received an amount of money from friends in the form of condolence gifts. We decided to donate it to the Atomic-Bomb Hospital in Hiroshima. I took the money there myself. Though I am one of the people exposed to the bomb's radiation, I had never been to this hospital before. The sight of so many people still suffering from incurable sicknesses caused by the bombing deeply saddened me and brought back with renewed freshness my own recollection of the experiences of our family.

In August, 1945, I was fourteen and a second-year student in a prefectural girls' high school. Because we were afraid that as the war approached a final and desperate stage we might be separated in a severe air raid, our family decided to hold a reunion on August 6 and to take a commemorative photograph of all of us together. My elder brother, then a member of a drafted corps assigned to an arsenal in Kure, took leave to come home for the occasion. My younger sister, evacuated to a temple in Kimita, returned; and my elder sister and I took a day off from the factory where we worked. The photographer was supposed to arrive at eight in the morning but was late for some reason. Consequently, we did not go into the garden, but stayed indoors occupying ourselves as we wished. The air-raid alarm had been lifted. We were even relieved to hear the sound of only one airplane flying over the city.

Suddenly a tremendous cracking sound nearly split my ear-drums. A pale blue flash temporarily blinded me; then total dark-ness enveloped everything. When the light once again penetrated the blackness, I saw the city of Hiroshima reduced to ruins.

In a vast area of flattened buildings, I could find only three standing: the Nihon Kangyo Bank in Kanayama-cho, the Fuku-ya Department Store, and our own two-story wooden house, by some miracle almost undamaged. Among the fallen timbers and over the shattered glass in the streets, people wandered to and fro.

The smell of fire was in the wind. Beyond the river, flames were already leaping up. Though we did not know what had happened, we had the presence of mind to check to make sure we were all together and to turn off the gas in the kitchen. Then, gathering what cooking implements, bandages, and medicines we could find, we left the house where we had lived for over a decade.

Fire now raged everywhere. A black rain fell, and dun smoke hid the sun. As we made our way to the Kyobashi River, whirl-winds tossed sheets of scorched galvanized iron along the streets. Then the winds struck the river, sending columns of water upward, dashing boats about, and heading directly for the place where we were standing. In terror, I dug a hole in the sand, crawled into it, and held my clothing to my body for fear it would be blown away. One whirlwind followed another raising clouds of sand that lashed at my back like countless needles. Unable to bear the winds any longer, we climbed to a piece of open land by the river. But the heat was so great that we were forced to enter the water of the river. Walking on dry land for even ten minutes was impossible because of the intense heat. We saw twenty or thirty people climb out of the water and then return several times. After a while, however, they seemed to have lost strength. Then they moved no more.

We spent the night by the river. The horror of the experience haunts me still. By morning, many of the people we had seen the

179

day before were dead. They lay on the shore or in water tanks and were so bloated that they scarcely looked like human beings. But all seven members of our family had survived. After caring for the burns my elder sister had suffered, we started up the river to Hesaka. All around, in contrast to the black rains and the sand-laden whirlwinds of the previous day, a blazing summer sun shone on the hellish, demolished city.

On all the bridges and roads lay charred corpses with staring white eyes and grinning mouths of white teeth. I saw them, but my mind was too blank to register terror. Soldiers with dangling arms, flayed skin, and yellowish substances oozing from eyeless sockets begged for water. There was nothing we could do. Besides, I doubt if any of us was in his right mind. The city was strangely silent.

Though we had been exposed, we were lucky. Later we suffered falling hair and bleeding gums and a long period of strange languor. But for three years we were able to live in a cottage in the compound of the house of a family for whom my father had long been family doctor. All of us seemed to have recovered completely.

Nonetheless, between the ages of twenty and twenty-nine, I suffered from a crushing series of illnesses: a chronic liver ailment for six years, pleurisy, pernicious anemia, gall-bladder trouble, and persistent and unidentifiable fever. Although, as a physician, my father was able to give me elaborate treatment at home, nothing seemed to help. I was told that I would probably spend the rest of my life in a sickbed and that I could never have children.

The prediction has proved false. I have lived a highly active life and have raised three sons. I believe that my good fortune and my vigorous life are owing to the strength I derive from my faith in Buddhism.

Hiroshima is now a vast modern city, but it stands on the corpses of the victims of the bombing. I am convinced that it is the duty of those of us who have survived to inspire everyone with whom we come into contact with a burning desire for peace.

Inertia Overcome

Kuniso Hatanaka

SOME MEN EXPERIENCE a downfall that resembles the down-
hill rolling of a ball. Just as inertia keeps the ball in motion
until the bottom of the slope has been reached, so fate seems to
keep the man descending until he reaches the nadir and finds a
place where he can stand firm, then start upward again. The
downfall of our family started on August 6, 1945.

Having been drafted into the army, I was stationed at Kochi at
the time. My wife and our two children and my elderly mother
were still at home in Hiroshima. On the morning of August 6, my
wife, three months pregnant, strapped our younger son, who was
only a little over one year old, on her back and left home to help a
neighborhood association relocate a house in part of an air-raid
safety program. Probably because he realized that heavy work
was too much for a pregnant woman carrying a small child, the
leader of the group asked my wife to guard the workers' lunches.
She went into the small nearby shed, where the lunches were. A
few seconds passed while the leader gave instructions. Then a
blinding flash struck. In the next instant, a pall of blackness fell,
obliterating everything. When she could at last make out her sur-
roundings, my wife was appalled. All around was total devastation. Our son was covered with blood; countless glass fragments
of all sizes were embedded in the flesh of his head. In a frantic
effort to find security, my wife, with our son still strapped to her
back, ran to and fro in the western part of the city. Soon black
rain fell. She took temporary shelter in a hut in a rice field.

Three days after the bomb blast, my family evacuated to my
wife's parents' home in Otake. About a week later, the effects of
radiation manifested themselves. All the hair fell from my wife's
head. Her entire body broke out in eruptions, her teeth became
loose, and bloody pus oozed from her gums. She coughed blood

181

and suffered with bloody stools. She was too weary to carry even the lightest thing the smallest distance. Her breasts no longer gave sufficient milk for our weeping infant, who suffered from radiation-caused diarrhea in addition to his other wounds. On the twenty-third day after the atomic-bomb blast, the small boy died. He is buried in a quiet cemetery in my home village. Though memorial services are held each year in Hiroshima for the victims of the bombing, no one visits my son's grave.

> On a hill in our village,
> my son sleeps,
> While Hiroshima memorials are held again.

As my wife was attempting to recuperate from her radiation-caused illness, the baby in her womb continued to develop. In February, 1946, a daughter was born to us. At the time, none of us could tell she was to be forever barely human.

The name the Ministry of Health and Welfare devised for my daughter's condition is "a syndrome caused by early prenatal, short-distance exposure to radiation." She is mentally retarded and microcephalic, with various complications. As the word microcephalic indicates, her head is far smaller than that of a normal child. Her condition was brought on by radiation exposure while she was in an early embryo stage. Ominously, at the time of her birth, the midwife said, "You will have to take special care of this baby."

At birth she weighed 1.9 kilograms. Both of her hip joints were dislocated. While giving the infant her first bath, the midwife noticed that her left leg was bent inward and that no amount of massage and stretching would put it right. As her first, then her second and third years passed without her being able to walk or speak, we gradually abandoned the hope that she was only somewhat retarded and, in 1952 and 1953, consulted a specialist from a team at the Hiroshima University School of Medicine, who diagnosed her condition as microcephaly. Doctors often told parents

182

that such children never live to be twenty. Our daughter is now over thirty but still cannot go to the toilet alone. She has the mentality of an infant of about two years and three months of age.

The atomic bomb brought my wife great suffering and created the tragedy of my microcephalic daughter. It also destroyed all my property, leaving us penniless. I am a barber, but at the time I had no money with which to open a shop and try to make a living. I borrowed a barber's chair and converted an ordinary room into a small shop, where I worked hard. But all our efforts proved futile. We had nothing. My small business failed. We were evicted.

After moving to Nishi Iwakuni, I contrived to open another barber shop. But once again, the inertia of my descent continued pulling me down. The shop failed, the landlord forced us to leave the shop, and wholesalers employed professional bill collectors to dun me. I pawned whatever I could, knowing that I would never be able to redeem the articles. There were six of us. In cold weather, we had to decide whether we wanted coal for the stove or rice to eat. We could not afford both. From 1957 to 1961, we struggled along at the lowest possible level. Then, one day I joined an important Buddhist organization and began to lead the life of faith that has helped me over the stony paths to a better way.

In 1965, I formed the Mushroom Society, an association of parents of microcephalic children whose condition was caused by the radiation of the Hiroshima bombing. I am once again operating a successful barbershop. My microcephalic daughter, far from being a burden, is indispensable to our happiness. Our fourth and youngest daughter is a great help to me in my work and to all of the family. Each year, when memorial services for the Hiroshima victims of the atomic bomb are held, my mind is filled with a thousand different emotions; but all of them are related to the sincere prayer that the world will one day know lasting peace and freedom from war.

Obligation To Testify

Atsuko Yamamoto

IN THE SUMMER OF 1945, I was working at a suburban factory as a member of the Student Patriotic Service Corps and was attending a girls' high school as a third-year student. I was fifteen. On August 6, I was on my way to school for classes. It was a Monday, a day on which electricity was not supplied to our factory. Walking near Hiroshima Station, I heard aircraft. I thought it was odd, since the all-clear had sounded earlier in the morning. As I looked up into the blue, cloudless sky, a tremendous light flashed. The force of a huge blast hurled me to the ground. When I came to, I felt something blazing hot on the back of my neck. The collar of the middy blouse of my school uniform was on fire. Quickly I put out the flames. My pantaloons — we all wore them during the war — had been burned away. Even my watch and shoes had been torn from me. I had nothing on but the rags of my blouse and my underwear. Assuming that a bomb must have made a direct hit nearby, I started running in the direction of home. But even as I began, throngs of blood-smeared, half-naked people rushed from the direction of my house. Something horrible must have happened there too.

I did not know what to do or where to turn. Looking around me, I saw a partly demolished streetcar. Inside stood scores of passengers, dead. Some of them still held in their hands the straps to which they had been clinging when the bomb exploded.

My confusion grew worse, and home was all I could think of. In spite of my fear of what I might find, I hurried along. Destroyed buildings blocked my way. Bleeding and injured people hurried from place to place calling for their children or parents. American planes still circled over a city that was now a sea of flame. Soon it began to rain great, greasy, black drops. On my way to the river, I had to walk over burning timbers and dead

184

bodies. The heat became unbearable. To cool myself, I jumped into the river, where the tide carried corpses past me. I pushed some of them aside to drink water to quench my scorching thirst. The tide ebbed. I slept on the beach among the dead.

When I wakened, I resumed my efforts to go home. But home existed no more. At least, I could not find it, for all the familiar landmarks had been destroyed. For three days, I dashed around Hiroshima in a frantic effort to escape the ever-pursuing flames.

On the fourth day, I found a train in operation and boarded it to join my mother, brothers, and sisters, who had been evacuated to the country earlier. When I arrived at the place where they were, I found everything in a shambles. I called out my name and cried for my mother; but I was afraid that even if she were there she would not know me. My face was burned black. My blouse was in tatters. I had on nothing else except a curtain that I had found and wrapped around my waist. Still, she did find me and recognize me. She and her neighbors took me to a hospital.

Daily after that, we traveled in a bicycle-drawn cart for treatment, though all that could be done was to apply Mercurochrome to my wounds and change the bandages. Other medicaments were unavailable. It took six months for the wounds to heal. How impatient I was for the day when the bandages would be removed.

When they were, mother would not let me near the mirror. Finally, however, I forced my way past her and saw myself. Weeping, I collapsed to the floor. I could not believe that it was my face.

My hands and feet were scarred with red welts. The fingers of my left hand were permanently bent at the joints. My face was covered with ugly keloidal scars. Until the bandages were off, I had cherished some hope. Now all hope was gone. How could I go on living with such a face? I cursed the war and my fate. I knew that there could be neither gods nor Buddhas in a universe where such things were allowed to happen.

My life became a crushing series of nightmarish incidents. I recall being sent to town on an errand one day. People turned their heads to stare at me; small children chased me and called me hurtful names. Humiliated, unable to complete the errand, I returned home weeping.

The face is of the greatest importance to a woman. With my scarred and hideous appearance, I despaired of life. One day, I took rat poison. But mother found out soon enough to give me treatment and prevent death. I had to go on, even though neither I nor any other person in the world could do anything about my face. Even my mother once let slip a painful remark: "What am I to do, saddled with a cripple like you for the rest of my life?"

If I was to live, I needed work. After some thought, I decided to learn dressmaking, which, once learned, could be done in the privacy of my home. But to learn the skill, I had to make a thirty-minute train ride each way to a school in the city. Alone, with no friends, I had to muster great courage for the daily trip. I was so embarrassed by the stares of the other passengers that in winter I covered my face with the kind of white gauze surgical mask that people often wear when they have colds. In summer, of course, I could not stand the heat with such a mask on.

In hot weather, other women can wear short-sleeved blouses. For ten years I wore long sleeves always, to hide my scarred arms. On the train people avoided me as if I were a monster. Sometimes I was so hurt that I would go to the train-car vestibule and weep in silence. After six months of commuting, I gave it up as too emotionally trying.

One day I read an advertisement for nurse trainees. Optimistically thinking that it would be fitting for an afflicted person like me to devote herself to the healing of others, I applied. But the person who conducted my interview humiliated me by saying that my appearance would be an obstruction to the recuperation of patients.

Finally, I found work that I could do and that was not odious to me. A relative of my eldest sister's husband, living in Hiroshima, wanted a maid to cook and do the laundry. In such a job, I would not have to meet many people and would live in relative seclusion. Working up my courage, I applied and took the job.

Some time later, a friend introduced me to a Christian church in the hope that religious life might offer me solace. Through the efforts of the pastor of the church, who was an American, I was sent to the United States to undergo plastic surgery. I lived in America for thirteen months. While there, I became friends with a widow who, having lost her husband in the war, was living in penury and solitude. I came to realize that I had been foolish to suffer alone. I was not the only unfortunate person in the world.

At last, aware of the need to be useful to my society, I returned to Japan, where an acquaintance helped me find work as a telephone operator. A man in the same office asked me to marry him. Later I gave birth to a girl. My husband and I built a new home, and I was very, very happy for seven years. But it was not to last. Ultimately, my husband and I were divorced. Our three-year-old daughter was left in my custody.

Once again, death seemed the only way to bring my suffering to an end. Taking my daughter with me, I went to a hot-spring resort in a remote mountain district. This time, I was determined that no one would interfere with my suicide. I put my daughter to sleep, then took sleeping tablets. While waiting for them to take effect, I intended to strangle my child. But looking at her sweet, innocent face, I could not harm her. Suddenly it dawned on me that if I had the courage to take my life I had the courage to live it. All I needed to do was harness my courage for positive and constructive purposes. I myself thwarted my third and final suicide attempt by quickly calling for medical assistance.

After some time had passed, I became acquainted with a devout Buddhist whose way of life impressed me. In November, 1965, I joined that person's Buddhist group — Nichiren Shoshu — and since I began living a life of faith I have been glad that I did not kill myself. Life is now a joy for me.

Four years ago, my daughter and I went to the United States to express gratitude to an elderly couple who had helped me

187

when I had lived a month in New York. Now I have fulfilled my long-cherished dream of opening a dressmaking shop of my own. I know that I have a moral obligation to tell my ordeal to as many people as possible. Once, my ugly scars made me dread social contacts. Today they are the testimony that I bear to young people to the effect that all war must be abolished.

Overcoming Suffering and Discrimination

Mihoko Takeuchi

I NEVER SAW the horrors of the war or of the Hiroshima bombing because I was not born until October 2, 1945. In my early childhood, it never dawned on me that I would ever suffer as an outcome of those horrors.

But in October, 1958, while I was rehearsing for a culture festival at the junior high school where I was a first-year student, I noticed red spots on my arms. I did not know what they were but felt convinced they would go away by themselves. They did not. And on the day of the culture festival, glancing in the mirror, I saw that my gums were coated with dark, coagulated blood. I was rushed to our family physician, who examined me at once and gave me an injection, which made me bleed so profusely that in no time the sleeve of my blouse was crimson. Grandmother, who had accompanied me, looked worried but attempted to calm me by saying it was only a rash of some kind. Her attempts were not successful. Terrified by something that I could not understand, I felt as if I were falling into a bottomless pit.

These alarming symptoms prompted me to ask my mother why I had been sent to the Atomic Bomb Casualty Commission yearly

188

since primary school. I had never understood the need for the checkups to which I was subjected there. My mother explained at last that at the time of the Hiroshima bombing, when eight months pregnant with me, she had been at a place only four kilometers from the hypocenter. Even when I was very small, red spots had appeared on my skin. Owing to the inability of our family physician to do anything about them, mother had gotten in touch with the Atomic Bomb Casualty Commission.

On the day after the school culture festival, a car came to take me to the commission for an examination. Terror struck me when I learned that instead of being allowed to go home at once I was to be hospitalized. I wept and pleaded with my mother: "It's only a rash, isn't it?" After a moment's silence, mother nodded reassuringly, patted me on the shoulder, and said, "You're going to be all right, dear. Don't worry." But her face was twisted with fear and grief.

My hospitalization and my struggle with my fate were a great trial for mother. Lying in bed, I asked myself why I should suffer such a destiny. What had I done to deserve this? I lamented and pitied myself. Often I was angry with my mother and, when she visited me, would either say hurtful things or maintain a sullen silence. I did this to help me forget, because, when the fear of death suddenly seized me, I wept hysterically. At such times, my mother could only stand by helplessly.

The red spots gradually disappeared; and after a little over a month, I left the hospital. Though pronounced cured, I was never free of the fear of a relapse and developed the habit of checking my arms and legs for red spots often. A few years passed safely. Then, one day in 1962, when I was a second-year student in a girls' high school, I discovered a red spot on my knee. Stunned, I scrutinized the rest of my body and found many more such spots. As had happened years earlier, my gums were coated with coagulated blood.

Back in the hospital, I was ordered to rest. Constant hemorrhage deprived me of appetite. I grew pale and had fainting spells.

I wasted away to a virtual skeleton, and my complexion turned ashen gray. Apprehensive of death every moment, I dreaded falling asleep at night for fear that I might never wake.

I was released from the hospital, but not from the horror of my life. From time to time, my condition became so unbearable that I wanted to kill myself. I could see no reason to continue to live with my illness. Once I went to a river intending to throw myself into it and drown. But as I stood on the brink, I saw a vision of my mother and grandmother and abandoned the idea. On another occasion, I climbed a mountain with the intention of jumping from a cliff, but another vision of my mother and grandmother stopped me.

Some time later, I pledged myself to a religious life and resolved not to give in to my sickness. I did not give in and am now living a fulfilled life, though I am still not in perfect health.

Physical suffering, however, is only one of the burdens that must be borne by the second and third generations of people affected by atomic-bomb radiation. In various circles in Nagasaki and Hiroshima, unjust discrimination is practiced against the children and grandchildren of the victims of the bombings. Consequently, many people conceal the fact that their parents or grandparents were victims because such information might damage their chances in work or marriage. People who develop symptoms of radiation-caused sickness tend to withdraw into themselves.

I understand how these people feel, but they must realize that a submissive attitude will only result in increased discrimination. I believe that the children of survivors of the atomic-bomb attacks must work together to protect their basic human rights and to promote peace.

Poisoned Before Birth

Yoshinori Yamashita

MY MOTHER was an ordinary woman, but she had great courage. When I was a child, she often told me that her aim was to work so that I and all other children like me would never have to go to war. Part of her struggle to this end was the organization of a study group of mothers of primary-school students to discuss the responsibilities and historical role of woman. I myself was a primary-school pupil when she started this group. But soon her activities expanded. She led street campaigns against the Japan-United States Security Treaty and against all war. At the many meetings conducted in our home, I was always amazed at mother's energy and devotion.

She was strict with us, and her example inspired us with social awareness at an early age. When a first-year student in junior high school, I wrote an essay on the existence of god. My teacher praised my work at a parent-teachers' meeting. I was elated by my own success, but mother severely warned me about being exultant over a small triumph.

Toward the end of the summer after my second year in middle school, I became listless and lost all appetite. A tumor developed on my neck. I was forced to go to a hospital for examinations. Mother went with me; and on the way home, as we trudged along in the dusk, she said over and over, as if to herself, "It isn't malignant. It can't be!" Terror gripped my heart, for I had heard of the fate of the so-called second generation of atomic-bomb victims.

I realized that I was one of them when I was hospitalized to undergo surgery on the tumor. The doctors said at the time that my days might be numbered. Mother sobbed bitterly when she learned this; and I overheard her tell someone that she should

191

never have eaten that apple, washed in the deadly black rain that fell on Hiroshima while I was still in her womb. My own fear was overwhelming, but I was nonetheless capable of realizing the immensity of her grief. She had struggled bravely to have war abolished for the sake of children; now one of her own children was in grave danger because of the effects of the atomic bomb.

I hovered on the borderline for a while; but I narrowly escaped death, and my condition gradually improved. A year later, to my mother's intense happiness, I was allowed to return to school. But at the beginning of each new school year, I was haunted by the fear that it might be my last.

One morning in my first year of high school, I went downstairs to find my father preparing to take mother to a hospital. Though I knew that she had not been feeling well, I had not suspected anything serious. But this was the start of her long, silent, painful fight for survival. She had cancer that required two operations. In spite of a condition that caused her to vomit blood from time to time, she never complained. All she said was, "To live involves pain."

Shortly after three in the afternoon, on June 16, 1964, she died. It was hot and stuffy that day. The palms of my hands would not stay dry. On the preceding night she had coughed up much blood and had made strange, choking sounds. An autopsy revealed that she had been strangled by blood accumulated in her windpipe. Her entire body was eaten away with diseases caused by the radiation to which she had been exposed in Hiroshima: lung cancer, liver cancer, uterine cancer, and others.

On the evening of the same day, we told grandmother of mother's death. Long bedridden with radiation-caused cancer, she only muttered weakly, "She was young. I should have died in her place." Ten days later, grandmother died, leaving only the three of us: my father, my younger brother, and me.

At the time of the deaths of my mother and grandmother, I had been expelled from high school because of delinquency. The social awareness and desire to improve the world that mother had tried to instill in us from early childhood had faded in the face of the constant fear of death from radiation-caused cancer. As if kicking back at my cursed fate, throughout high school I lived a life of quarrels and dissipation.

Three months after my mother's death, I fled Hiroshima because I could no longer tolerate existence there. I went to Tokyo, where I found things no better.

I continued a life of dissolute behavior but read voraciously in the hope of finding a reason for living, a definition of the meaning of life and death. I found none and contemplated suicide.

I reentered high school in Tokyo because I wanted to make a fresh start. Still, mental agony plagued me. I was fond of studying and speaking English at the time. One day in a coffee shop frequented by foreigners I happened to meet a Canadian woman who listened attentively to my story. When I finished speaking, she took a newspaper clipping from her handbag and gave it to me to read. It was entitled "Former Delinquent Boy Becomes Number-one Social Leader." The article frequently employed the word *faith*, which surprised me. Seeing this, the Canadian woman began to talk with me in earnest. Her story lasted for three hours, during which time she made every effort to convince me that it was my duty and mission to try to carry on my mother's antiwar campaign. I trembled with excitement at what she told me.

Returning exhausted to my boardinghouse, I picked up a book I had borrowed from a friend. On the first page, a passage struck me with great impact: "War is barbarous and inhuman. Nothing is more cruel, nothing more tragic."

That book was the first volume of *The Human Revolution*, by Daisaku Ikeda, a man fervently devoted to promoting the happiness of all peoples. A week after reading the book, on February 27, 1966, I joined a large Buddhist organization and began a life of religious faith that changed everything for me. Although in the

193

past, I was too ashamed and grieved by my destiny to write openly about it, faith in the Law of the Buddha has led me to try to improve myself and to share my experiences in the hope of helping others.

What We Have Done
Part 2

And there followed hail and fire mingled with blood,
and they were cast upon the earth:
and the third part of trees was burnt up,
and all green grass was burnt up.

REVELATION 8:7

On the First Rescue Train
Mankichi Matsuyama

IN THE LAST months of the war, when things were going badly for Japan and when American bombers constantly filled the skies, all Japanese people were training and preparing themselves for the ultimate battle that was expected to take place on the home islands. At the time, I was assistant chief of the Nagasaki conductors' station of the Japanese National Railways. We were very busy transporting war supplies. My family and I had evacuated to a house in the suburbs of the city, where we felt safer.

I was on duty until nine in the morning on August 9, 1945. After handing over the job to the shift that followed us, I headed home on the ten-forty train from Nagasaki Station.

On the way to Nagayo Station, after Michino Station, we saw a terrible flash. Then a tremendous blast almost threw me from my seat. The train ground to a halt. Passengers had been blown about inside the coach. Many were wounded and bleeding from the glass that flew everywhere when all the windows were blown out. I immediately offered to help the crew, and we drove the train to Nagayo. At the station, we ordered all the passengers to detrain. With the assistance of the station staff, we gave medical aid to the wounded and learned that the entire city of Nagasaki was in flames because of an air raid. Countless people had been killed or injured.

The railway authorities hastily decided to make an all-out ef-

197

fort to save as many people as possible. A train then standing in the station was converted into the first emergency-rescue train for Nagasaki.

But we had heard such horrible stories of conditions in the city that we resolved first to send a motor car along the line to find out whether the way was clear. I drove the car; with me were five people from the control and rail-maintenance departments. As we approached Michino Station, we saw huge clouds of black smoke swirling upward from the direction of Nagasaki. Our hearts sank as we watched the smoke, increasing by the minute and clearly indicating what must be happening in the city.

The windows of the station building at Michino had all been smashed. The walls were largely destroyed. The staff was trying to clear up as much of the debris as they could, while wiping away the blood streaming from wounds on their faces and bodies.

We did not remain long in Michino but continued our reconnaissance. The minute we turned the curve just out of Michino, we were confronted with a thick curtain of black smoke from which shot columns of flame. Not a building remained standing. In the direction of Ohashi, nothing was visible except the blanket of smoke. The bomb that had fallen on Nagasaki could not be a conventional one. We moved very slowly, since visibility grew worse and since the rail-maintenance men had to remove electrical cables that had fallen and were hanging across the tracks.

Long files of victims walked by us on the sides of the tracks. Burned, half-naked, shocked, they moved along in spite of everything, supported only by the strength of the human will to survive. Some were so charred that their sexes were difficult to determine. We called to them that a rescue train would come soon, but they showed almost no reaction.

We continued toward Ohashi Bridge, but when we moved to a point about halfway between Nishimachi and Ohashi, we sensed danger. Gas was leaking from a huge tank in the vicinity. Getting down from the car, I walked toward the site of the bridge. There was nothing there except massive, grotesquely twisted steel

198

supports projecting from the water. The bridge itself was gone. The railway ties were on fire. We headed back to Nagayo because we could go no farther in this direction.

At Michino, we met the rescue train and started relief work. The locomotive pushed the coaches from behind while the conductor blew the train whistle as a signal. Victims grew more numerous closer to the city, and the coaches quickly filled. The injured did not want to sit on the benches. If there had been room, they would have preferred to lie on the hard, wooden floor.

Near Ohashi, a young man ran toward us shouting, "My wife's trapped under a pile of burning lumber. Please help her!' Although we gave no thought to ourselves, we had so many refugees and so many more were coming every minute that it was impossible to stop to do anything for the young man or his wife. From the flames, the shelters, the swirling smoke, we heard people crying for water and for assistance. If this was not hell, what was it?

The wounded that we transported were taken to the naval hospital at Isahaya, but I learned that almost all of them died soon. After August 12, we transported fewer wounded and more unrecognizable, burned corpses.

On the night of August 9, American bombers dropped leaflets appealing to us to surrender. Reading a leaflet, I learned for the first time that an atomic bomb of dreadful destructive power had been dropped on Nagasaki. The leaflet claimed that all living creatures in the bombed area would perish and that nothing would grow there for seventy years. The tension that had supported me in the trying days of the war and that had preserved in me hope of a turn for the better vanished. I shuddered, and a passionate longing for a termination to the war flooded my whole body. Six days after the bombing of Nagasaki, I heard the emperor's radio broadcast announcing the unconditional surrender of Japan. I was still engaged in rescue operations at the time.

A single atomic bomb killed 74,000 people, injured 75,000 more, and destroyed 18,000 buildings. Nor is this the end of the list of casualties. Tens of thousands of people who received no external injury soon fell victims to radiation sickness. Many of them died very soon. Three decades after the bombing, countless victims still suffer the aftereffects of radiation exposure, and some of them die every year.

Double Death Sentence
Shigetaka Iwanaga

WHEN THE BOMB exploded over Nagasaki, on August 9, 1945, I was a member of the military police and was in charge of accounts and inspections of war supplies and civilian aid-defense shelters. Inspecting the shelters, my main work, was part of a program to remodel the facilities and enable them to withstand flame-thrower attacks in the event that United States troops landed on the home islands.

I was conducting one of these inspections when the atomic bomb fell. Soon people of both sexes and of all ages, some clothed, some naked, hurried into the shelter and almost at once fell dead. Corpses practically clogged the entrance. Sensing the danger of remaining in such a place, I began to wade through the dead bodies toward the exit. There I found still more mounds of corpses.

Upon escaping the shelter, I first went to the Shiroyama Commercial School, in the auditorium of which were stored three years' provisions for the civilian population. The building and the provisions were in flames when I arrived. Many of the soldiers who had been hastily mobilized to save what they could from the fire were seriously wounded. Still other injured soldiers were dissolving powdered milk in a large cauldron and doling it out to the refugees who had come seeking food.

200

For some reason, that evening, another soldier and I were walking behind the Shiroyama Primary School when we heard women
crying from a small river. Descending to the bank, we saw three
naked, injured people. To my horror, I realized that they were
three sisters I had known. One of them had her small children
with her. I lifted the edlest sister to my comrade, who remained
on the bank. I saw that her eyes had been burned out and that
she was blistered all over. When I touched her, the skin peeled
off, causing her such pain that she cringed from me. After much
careful and laborious work, we succeeded in getting them to the
relief squad.

Later, I was forced to go to a special guard and police headquarters in Naminohira to report on the situation in Shiroyama-
machi. The Urakami River and the Komaba Bridge over it were
clogged with dead bodies. When I reached it, the bridge was already burning. There was nothing for me to do but push my way
through the corpse-choked waters of the river. Carrying my
sword and tying my cap on my head with a towel, I ran as fast as I
could, in rubber-soled shoes.

As I went along, I heard people pleading for water. Today, I
can still hear their cries and feel remorse at having been unable to
do anything to relieve them. We had been ordered not to give
water to the injured because it would only hasten death. Forcing
myself not to hear their cries, occasionally stumbling over the
dying, I hastened on my way.

As I raced on, I suddenly experienced a strange delusion. The
flames of the city reminded me of the time when I had taken part
in the Japanese amphibious assault on the Chinese coast during
the Shanghai Incident of 1937. The inferno in the streets of Nagasaki suddenly became the flames of Shanghai, until the urgent
cries of the Japanese around me brought me back to reality.

Near the police box at Ibinokuchi, I saw a dead baby and, not
far away, its injured mother, who was screaming and desperately
trying to crawl to her child's side. I picked up the little corpse and
placed it by the mother, who died almost immediately. Weeping

201

aloud and vowing to get even some day, I ran farther. Just as I came to a cotton mill, where in the past I had seen American prisoners of war working, I stopped, terrified as the walls of the building tumbled in flames into the street that I would have been passing if I had not stopped with the dead infant and dying mother. In their deaths they had saved my life.

Approaching my final destination, I found the heat from the roaring flames so intense that I was forced to pour water over my body to continue. Tangled fallen wires tripped me at every step. Only my sense of mission made me go on. Ultimately, I reached the Tamae Bridge, where the fire was less intense, and then continued to the headquarters, where I made my report.

My duty done, I suddenly felt crippling pain in my feet. Examining them for the first time, I saw that the rubber soles of my shoes had burned away and that my feet were stuck with countless glass splinters. My whole body ached. My clothes were in rags. There was no medical team at the headquarters, but in the supply room I managed to get some iodine and some clothes and shoes.

I spite of the pain in my cut and burned feet, I still had to work. I was assigned several tasks, including guarding Nagasaki Station, disposal of corpses, and cremation. Later I guarded Emmyo-ji—ironically, the Temple of Survival—where wounded, most of whom died, were taken. I was enraged and indignant as I watched innocent, noncombatant, unarmed civilians suffer and perish. What had they done to deserve this?

Another of my jobs was checking people leaving the city, helping the elderly and children, and preventing able-bodied young people from fleeing. In one instance, it was my duty to force a young man with a bundle to return to the destroyed city.

Before long, I found myself under a double death sentence. Rumors were rife at the time that anyone who lost hair or suffered from bleeding gums was doomed to die of radiation sickness. I had lost some hair, and blood oozed from my gums. Then, after the surrender, word leaked out that all members of the military police were to be hanged.

202

The latter rumor proved false first. Before long I was discharged from military service, and no blame was laid on me. But the sentence of death from radiation sickness still hung over my head. Shame and humiliation accompanied me on my return to my home village. To be prepared if suicide should become inescapable, I always carried a sword, wrapped in a blanket.

My health deteriorated because of a strange, persistent fever that the doctors found impossible to identify. After a period of great suffering, I recalled eating mugwort to cure a high malarial fever contracted while I had been in China. Instinct must have led me to eat the herb that time. I decided to try again. Every day I ate some of the mugwort that grew in my village. In a fairly short time, my gums stopped bleeding; and even sharp tugging would not pull my hair out. I began to feel better, the fever subsided, and I regained the will to live.

The second death sentence had been lifted. Throughout the decades that have passed, I have continued to pray for the repose of those who died in the Nagasaki holocaust.

Hopeless Attempts to Help
Kakuji Miyazaki

"BY SUMMER, I'll be taller than you, father," calls my sixteen-year-old son, as he measures his height against mine. He has a voracious appetite, grows at an amazing rate, and studies hard. He is happy. When I was sixteen, the war prevented my studying and forced me to work in a munitions factory. When I was sixteen, the world's second atomic bomb fell on Nagasaki.

Though a student at the Nagasaki Normal School, I worked at the Mitsubishi Arms Plant. Our labor was exhausting, but we did our duty with all our might, in the hope that the tide of the war would change in our favor and enable us to defeat the Allies.

On August 9, 1945, at the beginning of lunch break, I went to the lavatory to wash my hands. As I was about to step out of the factory door, there was a tremendous flash. Instinctively I dodged back into the building and was about to take cover when a sky-splitting, deafening blast hurled me to the floor.

After some seconds—I cannot say how many—I peeped through my hands. Though the day had been bright and sunny, everything was now as dark as if it were twilight. I heard anguished cries for help from all sides. The factory ceiling had collapsed. The walls had been blown away. In the chaos and destruction, injured factory workers lay everywhere.

Rushing outside, I saw to my still greater horror that the factory compound was a wasteland. Most of the buildings had been leveled. The ground was littered with twisted objects, shattered glass, and dead and dying human beings disfigured beyond recognition.

The end of the world! Terrified and stunned, I began to flee in the direction of the hills where there were well-protected shelters. A turmoil of refugees clogged the streets. People whose skin hung from them like rags and whose bodies were so burned that it was impossible to tell their sexes screamed for help. Running in all directions, everyone had but one thought: escape.

As if trying to free myself from the monstrosity of what I saw and heard, I ran as fast as I could. As I ran, I realized that the destruction must have been caused by another bomb like the one that had fallen on Hiroshima a few days earlier.

When I reached the hillside, I found all the shelters overflowing with refugees. For want of a better place, I took refuge in a nearby potato field surrounded by trees. Soon some of my schoolmates arrived and told me that our school was on fire. Looking in the direction of the school, which was not too far away, I saw flames shooting from the dormitory building.

Struggling to my feet, I ran toward the dormitory to try to do something to help the many students I knew must be trapped

204

there. When I reached the school, I found only ten people engaged in the hopeless task of trying to extinguish the fire.

Students were trapped under the partially collapsed two-story wooden building. An older student whom I knew was crying for help. He had been pinned under a fallen ceiling beam. His body had burst open, and his internal organs were spilling out. One of our teachers lay motionless on the ground. Some students whose clothes had caught fire plunged into a nearby pond. Others were so burned that their raw, bleeding flesh was exposed.

We abandoned hope of putting out the fire and, working in a constant shower of sparks, tried to save as many people as possible. I used my gaiters for bandages. I lifted debris to free a student pinned under it. But there were so many! Then the entire dormitory was engulfed in flames. We had to leave the rest of the trapped boys to perish. Silently, I prayed for the repose of their souls. Their cries haunt me still.

We returned to the hill. In the evening began a ghostly, hellish parade of the wounded. Naked, burned, flayed, and bleeding they came. It was impossible to know whether some of them were men or women. One man glittered with countless slivers of glass embedded in his body. One attempted to keep his internal organs inside his split body with his hand. A mother, aimlessly wandering with a vacant expression on her face, held her dead child in her arms. Throughout the crowd ran other people in search of their relatives and loved ones. Their frenzied calls for mother, father, children, wives, and husbands echoed over the hillside.

Those of us who were not seriously injured did what we could to relieve the pain of the others, but all we had for medicine was pumpkin juice. By night, we had found some rice, which we cooked. With sweaty, blood-covered hands, we made balls of steamed rice for the injured. Because of the American reconnaissance planes overhead, we had to keep the cooking fire well covered.

The relief work in which I engaged from the following day took me throughout the Urakami Valley and into the very center of the bombed area. Unfortunately, not long afterward, I stepped on a nail and wounded my foot. The wound festered so badly that I was no longer in a condition to work. I decided to return to my home town of Minami Takagi. My arrival there four days later caused my family great happiness. Knowing that I had been in Nagasaki at the time of the bombing, they had given me up for dead.

Of all the vivid recollections I have of the horror of those days, one stands out from all the others. The wife and three children of Professor Shin'ichi Morita, one of our teachers at the normal school and later head of the Department of Education of Nagasaki University, were killed in the bombing. In spite of his personal grief, he directed extensive rescue work, carrying the cremated remains of his loved ones with him in a milk can.

In 1948, I began my career as a teacher by being assigned to the Chijimyo First Primary School. Later I was to teach at four other Nagasaki schools; but in 1950, I started manifesting symptoms of radiation sickness. My gums bled. I suffered from acute anemia, fainting spells, and apathy. My white-blood-cell count dropped drastically. Sapped of strength, I tired easily. If I worked or studied at night, my eyes became bloodshot and swollen. My days were darkened by dread of the disease.

But I went on with my teaching and tried to instill in my pupils respect for peace and hatred for the miseries of war. I did not succumb to the sickness; and in March, 1967, I stopped teaching, after twenty years in the profession, to enter the field of politics, where I hoped to contribute to the establishment of lasting peace.

In 1972, I introduced to the Nagasaki municipal assembly a motion for the establishment of an annual Peace Week between August 6 and 15. The motion was passed; and for a number of years Peace Week ceremonies, with special prayers for the victims of the atomic bombings, have been important annual events in both Hiroshima and Nagasaki. In themselves the ceremonies might seem insignificant, but I hope they will become part of the groundwork for the worldwide abolition of warfare.

Sad Reunion
Masaki Morimoto

AT NINE IN THE MORNING on that hot, humid day, some friends
and I went for a swim in a nearby irrigation pond. There were
ten of us, all about the same age. We splashed around in the cool
water until we became tired and hungry and decided to go home.
By twos and threes, we started for the bank. Then one of the
group shouted, "Hey, come and look! They're dropping a parachute bomb." All of us hurried out of curiosity to see what a parachute bomb was. Then we spotted something dangling from three
clustered parachutes hovering over Nagasaki Shipyard but heading our way.

Suddenly a white flash struck, and I fell. The last thing I remember before losing consciousness was the feeling of the grass
on the bank pressing against my forehead.

I had been lucky. I was blown off my feet, down the bank, and
into the water. The parts of my body that were in the pond were
neither seriously injured nor burned. I would have died like the
others, if I had been exposed to as much radiation as they.

Still I was not unhurt. The front of my body was so burned
that when I touched my chest the skin adhered to my palm and
pulled away. Climbing to the bank, I saw that my friends were all
alive, though they had been burned. Their hair was frizzled, and
they no longer had eyebrows. The tattered clothes of one badly
burned boy stuck fast to his inflamed skin. In less than a week,
seven of the ten had already died of radiation sickness.

Hurrying home, I found our house and all the other buildings
in the neighborhood blown to bits. Everyone who could walk or
crawl was fleeing to a large air-raid shelter near our house. I
joined the group, overtaking several seriously burned people who
were forced to go on all fours. Inside the shelter, I lay down and
watched as other victims rapidly filled the space. They were all

in pitiable condition. The eyeballs had been blown out of the sockets of one man's head. Before long, maggots hatched there and wriggled in the gaping holes. The burns on my own body festered and became infested with maggots. They were soon joined by some of the many swarms of flies prevalent that summer. Suppuration gradually spread to other parts of my body. More pus for the increasing numbers of maggots and flies. *Hell* is the only word to describe what we suffered. But soon, I had undergone so much that I became apathetic. The sight of the disfigured bodies of my friends left me unmoved.

Though I had not died in the bombing, I felt certain that in my wretched state, the end was not far away. For a month, I hovered between life and death. And then, one day my father managed to obtain a certain herbal medicine, which worked amazing improvements in my condition.

Our school reopened in borrowed quarters in October, 1945; and I was well enough to attend. Only forty of the former nearly two thousand pupils appeared the first day. In the spring of 1946, fourteen members of our class finished the sixth grade and entered middle school.

Two of my elder sisters were injured in the bombing. The oldest, who had carried me on her back to the hospital for treatment while I was still in grave condition, sustained severe burns but seemed to be doing well until the summer of 1946, when she died of radiation sickness. My other older sister, who had suffered no serious external injuries, died in 1951, of leukemia.

In 1968, we held a reunion of the group that had graduated from the sixth grade in 1946. Only nine of us had survived. Five had died, one after another, from various symptoms of the atomic disease. The American National Broadcasting Company television division filmed the reunion, which was later shown over a national network.

The meeting was a sad one. We had lost most of our childhood friends, but we still treasure the ones who remain, for we must try to encourage each other to go on.

Helpless

Kimiko Tanaka

JULY AND AUGUST are hot. The midsummer sun beats down mercilessly on all living creatures. At such times, I find it difficult to get out of bed. My room is stifling. Perspiration drenches my underclothes, and I am reminded of the day the atomic bomb was dropped on Nagasaki. I was twenty-eight and was living at Shiroyama, about nine hundred meters from the hypocenter.

Everything around me was scorched, desolate. Blackened, grotesquely disfigured corpses lay strewn on the ground. They emitted a foul, low-hanging stench. Some people, not quite dead, twitched their arms and legs and cried for water. The river was thick with bloated bodies floating toward the sea. The wind carried ghastly odors. Still today, indelible recollections of these things send a shudder through my whole body.

On the morning of August 9, 1945, thinking that, since the air-raid alert was over, I would wash and prepare some noodles for breakfast, I went into the garden for water. As I dipped a ladle in a large earthenware jug, something blinding flashed overhead. The impact of the explosion hurled me into the water in the storage jug. I pulled myself out, to see a yellow haze and smoke billowing into the sky. Suddenly something struck a hammer blow to the back of my head. I was aware of losing consciousness and of a burning sensation, as if my body were being seared by a sheet of red-hot iron.

I do not know how many hours passed before I regained consciousness. But the first thing I did was to try to find my son Isao, who was only two and a half years old. He had been playing with my husband's mother a little while before I had been struck unconsious.

In the immediate neighborhood had lived many of our relatives. My son and I lived with my mother. Next door was the

209

house of my younger brother and his wife; and my husband's mother and her married grandson lived not far away. The bomb had completely flattened the homes of these people and all the other buildings for as far as I could see in the swirling smoke.

The first person I found was my mother, roasted and completely bald, but still alive. Next I discovered my sister. Blood spurted from a cleft in her head that looked as if it might have been made with an ax. But she too was still alive.

Placing my hands on my own head, in an instant I found myself clutching all my hair, which had come off as if it had been a wig. Still, I was more fortunate than many. My younger brother, who had been working in front of a nearby cattle shed, was dead, armless and still standing. His wife lay sprawled on the earthen floor of a room in the wreckage of her house. Her body had been cut in two.

Nowhere could I find my son. I discovered my husband's mother. The blast had blown her a distance of ten meters. But still I could not locate Isao.

After five hours, during which my grievously injured mother and sister joined me in the search, we finally found my child under a pile of debris, lying with his head beside a stone mortar. He was alive; but his body was covered with burns and cuts, and the back of his head was virtually smashed in. Only two years old.

Lifting him gently, I started for the Urakami River, which flowed nearby. I wanted to wash him. On the way, I saw two little boys, brothers, who had lived near us. They had probably been playing on the bridge when the blast struck. They still stood there clinging to the rails. Their faces were burned beyond recognition. In agony they pleaded with me to help them. I wanted to give them assistance. But I was carrying Isao, for whom I had to find medical help. All I could say as I looked in their pleading eyes was, "Forgive me. There is nothing I can do."

When Isao regained consciousness the following day, he asked whether the air-raid alert had ended.

In the chaotic days following the bombing, medicine and doc-

210

tors were unavailable. I tried to care for Isao myself; but in about two weeks the back of his head was a mass of rotting flesh, bone fragments, and pus. Frantic, I went to Oita Prefecture to ask for help from my relatives. They turned a deaf ear to my entreaties when they learned that I was short of money. Having accomplished nothing, I returned to Nagasaki.

While I was in Oita, my husband, an army surgeon, visited me. I was bald, and the burns I had suffered had made my mouth look like a pig snout. My appearance must have shocked him greatly. Though he promised to return for me soon, I never saw or heard from him again. Not only did the accursed bomb kill, it also severed bonds among the living.

My son's condition grew steadily worse. Pain forced him to call out to me for relief. I was helpless. I could not even provide good things for him to eat. Food was too scarce. Often I longed to take his sufferings upon myself. I contemplated holding him in my arms and jumping in front of an oncoming train. But always a little spark of hope for his recovery prevented my doing anything drastic. But my hope was to be betrayed. On February 14, 1946, as I begged him to forgive my inability to do anything for him, my son died.

That same year, my mother died. My sister lived on for another fifteen years.

My own existence became one of continual trial. My hair had all fallen out, my gums bled, and I lost so much weight that I looked like a living skeleton. Still, I survived. What made me cling to life? A sense of mission to inform all the peoples of the world of the horrors caused by the atomic bomb. This is the only way I can take revenge against both the war and the bomb for wrecking my life and for taking the lives of my son, my mother, my brother, and my sister.

Hellish Years
After Hellish Days
Toyomi Hashimoto

THOUGH AT EACH anniversary the skies over our city are blue and peaceful, the memory of that day in 1945 still troubles my body and soul.

In spite of the wartime conditions, my husband and our little son and I lived a happy life. Many of our neighbors envied us. On the morning of August 9, 1945, I walked to the gate to see my husband off to work. My three-year-old boy, Takashi, went out to play with some of his little friends. I was alone in the house and relieved that the air-raid alarm had just been lifted.

Then, in the distance I heard an approaching airplane. "Japanese?" I wondered. I stepped outside to see my son running to me, calling, "Airplane! Airplane!" The moment we reentered the house, there was a blinding flash followed by a tremendous explosion. The roof of the house caved in, pinning us under a mountain of debris.

Hours passed. I do not know how many. Then I heard my son crying softly and calling for mother and father. He was alive. I tried to reach for him, but a huge beam imobilized me. I could not break free. Though I screamed for help, no one came. Soon I heard voices calling names of neighbors.

My son was bravely trying to crawl from under a heap of clay that had been one of the walls. His back was turned to me. When he faced me, I saw that his right eye was obliterated with blood. Once again, I tried to move, but the beam would not budge.

I screamed so loud and long that I must have lost my voice. I called to the people I could see scurrying about, but they did not hear me. No one answered until the lady next door finally pulled my son out of the wreckage.

212

Happy that he was at least temporarily safe, I suddenly became aware of a sharp pain in my breast, left hand, and stomach. With my free right hand I grabbed a piece of roofing tile and scraped away the dirt covering my breast. I could breathe more easily. As I tried again to crawl out, I saw that a huge nail was stuck in my stomach.

"Fire! Fire!" I could hear people shouting around me. It was either break free or burn to death. With a violent wrench, I pulled myself from under the beam. In doing so, I ripped the flesh of my stomach. Blood spurted from an agonizing gash in my body.

I was at last out of the ruined house. Still, my son was nowhere to be seen. Perhaps the kind lady next door had led him to safety. I had to search for him, but I could only limp slowly because of the pain in my stomach.

I decided to go to a nearby hill, which was open and might offer some security. As I crept slowly along, people more seriously injured than I clutched at my feet and pleaded for help and water. Among the piteous cries I heard loud voices shouting, "Leave the old people! Help the children first." I wanted to help, but I was in grave need of assistance myself. All I could do was promise to come back with water, if it was possible.

On my way to the hill, I met a neighbor and friend. Looking long and intently at me, she finally said, "It is Toyomi, isn't it?" I knew that my dress was in tatters and that I was bloody and dirty. But now, stopping to examine myself for the first time, I learned worse. One of my ears had been cut nearly off. It and my whole face were caked with congealed blood.

"Thank heaven you're alive!" I heard a familiar voice saying. Turning, with intense happiness, I saw my husband, who was holding our son in his arms. We climbed to the top of the hill together, walking among countless corpses.

On the hilltop, a kind man gave us bed sheets, candles, sugar, and other useful things. At once we began to try to do something for Takashi, who had lost consciousness. After a while, as we dripped sugar water into his mouth, he awakened.

He had already lost the sight of his right eye. Myriad slivers of glass were embedded in his head, face, body, arms, and legs. An air-raid alarm, still in effect, prohibited lighting candles. In the pitch darkness, my husband and I picked out as many pieces of glass from his body as we could find. So full of life and energy until that moment! Now blind in one eye and covered with blood and dirt! Still he bore everything bravely and only asked, "Am I being a good boy?" Pride at his courage and grief for his pain forced us both to weep quietly.

I made bandages from the bed sheet. Placing some boards over two large rocks, I made us a shelter. We were fortunate to be together. In the dark, we could hear people calling the names of their loved ones. I wondered what had happened to my younger and elder sisters.

The light of dawn showed us a hell. Corpses, some burned to cinders, others only partly roasted, lay everywhere. Barely living, faintly breathing, others rapidly drew toward death. A horrible stench filled the air.

In a few days we were taken to a bomb shelter where, in spite of a food shortage, we managed to live for a month. I was in such pain that it was excruciating to carry my son to the toilet. Nonetheless, he and I went daily to a nearby clinic for treatment. As days passed, my hair began falling; and blood oozed from my gums. My husband was too ill to walk. We began hearing rumors that the bomb that had destroyed Nagasaki was of the same kind as the one that had fallen on Hiroshima. People who had not been injured in the blast began to die, one after another. We waited for our turns to come.

Near the well from which we had to draw all our water corpses were cremated. On our way to the well, we had to pick a ghoulish way through a field of human bones. Often in the morning there would be a dead body by the well that had not been there the evening before. I wondered who would take care of our corpses when we died.

But we did not die. In September, my two drafted brothers

214

returned from the war. My younger and elder sisters turned up, safe and well. In October, we rented the house in Oura where I live with my family today.

In about a year, I began noticing purple spots on my body. I tired easily and suffered occasional sharp pains in the head. I learned that my white-blood-corpuscle count had dropped drastically. Aware that all these symptoms characterized the atomic diseases, I became apprehensive about my future. My husband was so ill that he could not work. By the time Takashi entered primary school, it was becoming difficult for us to make ends meet. Nor was our son's lot in school easy. Cruel neighborhood children hurt him deeply when they jeered and called him a one-eyed devil.

A single bomb had wrecked a peaceful and happy family. True, my husband had not gone to the battle front, but we were nonetheless as much victims of the war as the survivors of soldiers who had died fighting. The government offered financial assistance to such people, but none to our kind. With rising anger, I often asked myself why they discriminated in this way.

To all these trials was soon added my husband's total desperation and determination to kill himself and our son so that I could try to find some happiness on my own. I had to guard him constantly. Even so, he succeeded in making a number of attempts to strangle himself and our son. When, in 1948, he was taken to the police by a neighbor who found him trying to hang himself in the garden, he collapsed on the floor, crying, "Let me die. I can't stand the agony of living any more."

Since he could not work, I had to support the family by serving in restaurants, nursing the sick, and doing whatever odd jobs I could find. Over the years, my determination to keep on going was strengthened by the births of two more children. Still, sometimes I too weakened and contemplated suicide. My work was arduous, and I was weak. Occasionally I fainted on the job.

But even this was not to be the limit of what I was to witness and endure. In 1952, four months after his birth, I noticed

215

something queer about one of my fourth son's eyes. I took him to an ophthalmologist, who diagnosed the case as cancer of the eye. Very rare. One case in ten thousand. He added that unless the eye was removed at once, the cancer would spread; the eye would eventually pop from its socket; and my son would die, withered like a blasted tree. I was too shocked and terrified to cry.

The same doctor recommended that I take my child to a university hospital for treatment. At first I hesitated. We had no money to pay for such care. But I could not sacrifice my son's life. Resolving to scrape together the funds somehow, I took him to a university clinic where the first doctor's diagnosis was confirmed and where I learned that without immediate surgery there was grave danger that the cancer would spread to the other eye. Even in the light of this knowledge, however, I could not consent to having my child's eye removed.

About fifteen months later, this same child began to cough in an odd way. I wanted to take him to a nearby hospital but could not: I owed them money. Instead, I took him to a smaller hospital some distance from our home. The doctor at first said it was only a neglected cold. But when the child got no better and I took him to the hospital again, I was told that it was diptheria and that he would have to be hospitalized at once at the Nagasaki Hospital. Where was I to get the money?

I asked my elder brother's wife for aid, but she was too short of funds. Nevertheless, she offered to lend me her own son's health insurance policy. Her boy was three, or about a year and a half younger than my fourth son. Though terrified that our insurance fraud would be discovered, I had no choice but to accept her proposal.

Now my son was able to have good medical treatment. Vaccines were tried for a while, but they soon failed to have effect. The doctor insisted on surgery. Though the operation was a success, it had been necessary to install a respiratory device in my son's throat. The device was covered with thick gauze, which had to be kept constantly moist. If it dried, phlegm would accu-

216

mulate and strangle the boy. Since there was no money to spend on private nurses, I had to stay by his bedside constantly. My younger sister offered to help me, but a few days of the gruelling routine exhausted her and made her ill. Late at night when the doctor made his rounds, he would try to cheer us: "Keep it up. You're doing a good job."

Finally, my child's condition improved. To my delight, he was to be released from the hospital. The time had come to remove the respiratory device. But the doctor who was in charge made a mistake and cut an artery in the throat. The day before he was to have come home, my son died, strangled on his own blood.

The doctor knelt by the bed, groaning for forgiveness. I blamed him. But recriminations would not bring my boy back to life. I had falsified the insurance papers and had no alternative but to remain silent. Upon arriving in the hospital room, my husband collapsed. Weeping bitterly, he blamed himself for being unable to earn money to support the family.

My fourth son died on May 10, 1945. On the nineteenth of the same month, I was given work as a scrub woman in the university hospital. My pay, five hundred yen a day, was barely enough for survival and left nothing for luxuries. When our eldest son was in the sixth grade, penury threatened to deprive him of the chance to participate in the school excursion marking the end of primary and the beginning of middle school. After consideration of our condition, his school allowed him to go on the trip free of charge. But because of my work, I could not see him off. Our next-door neighbor was kind enough to do it for me.

My happiness at the birth of our fifth son, in June, 1956, was to be short-lived. I had hoped he would be a reincarnation of the baby I had lost. And in the most tragic and ironic way, he inherited the same eye disease that had afflicted his dead elder brother.

Why? My husband was a good, kind, gentle man. No one could speak ill of him. I had done no one wrong. I had always tried to be kind to the weak and the elderly. I was considered an excellent mother and housewife. Why, among my five brothers and sisters, had I been singled out for this suffering? My fequent and repeated prayers at Buddhist temples and Shinto shrines had no effect. The white film covering my son's eye was permanent. So deep was our physical and spiritual desolation at the time that the whole family agreed to commit suicide if it should become necessary to hospitalize this little boy.

My husband did not wait for the rest of us. His final suicide attempt left him ill and broken. Once again, there was no money. I pleaded with municipal officials, telling them how my husband's weakened physical state prohibited his working. I explained his history to them and said that I earned only the smallest income as a scrub woman. Finally, they agreed to provide him free hospital care and to put our family on government relief. Our condition had improved a little. But after about three months in a hospital bed, quietly, peacefully, my husband died in his sleep.

Though we did not know it then, our worst trials were over. My eldest son, limited by partial blindness, could not choose an occupation freely. He apprenticed himself to a shoemaker. I continued to work hard in the hope of providing a better future for the other children. Almost before I knew it, three years had passed; and I had been given a chance to remarry.

My second husband, who is crippled in both legs, is a skilled carver of tortoise-shell ornaments. As my children grew up, they earned money and contributed to the general fund so that little by little we were able to buy electrical appliances and ultimately to live an average family life on my husband's earnings alone.

Takashi, my oldest child, in spite of the loss of an eye, now works for a transport company and is the father of two lovely children. Immediately before he entered primary school, a doctor who gave him a physical examination told me that my fifth son's eye cancer had stabilized and would spread no farther. At the time of writing this, he was a senior in high school.

Though we have suffered, our family has, at least in part, survived. There are many others for whom the atomic-bomb sickness remains a constant source of pain and despair or an ever-present threat. Only people who suffer from this kind of illness can know its full terror. Even doctors do not always diagnose it accurately.

Young people today have been fortunate enough never to experience war. But they must not forget. It is the duty of those of us who have lived through the hells of the atomic bombings and the years of agony following them to proclaim our experiences so that war and its evils can be recognized for what they are and abolished from the earth.

Proof of My Death

Komaichi Taniyama

IN SPITE OF THE unfavorable course of the fighting, during the last days of World War II, when I was employed in the oxygen-torpedo section of the Mitsubishi Arms Plant, we worked diligently, secure in the belief that ultimately we would win. Many of the people in our department were women who wore white bands with the red rising-sun emblem on their foreheads to show that they were members of the Patriotic Service Corps and the Volunteer Corps.

On August 9, 1945, our day began, as usual, with a pep talk from the factory director. When it was over, we all turned to our tasks. At about nine-thirty, I heard a siren for an air-raid alert. Going immediately to the watchtower on the roof, I began to scan with binoculars. In the partly clouded sky, I could not see a single aircraft. The caution alert sounded, and I went back to work. It was swelteringly hot in the factory. We all sweated copiously.

Shortly after eleven, we were about to hoist and move a torpedo we had just assembled when suddenly something brilliant—something like lightning—flashed. My first reaction was

219

to look up to the high-voltage cable to see whether it had made contact with something. No, it was all right. I looked out the windows on the left and right. In the next instant, another flash blinded me; and heat waves enveloped everything. Quickly, I covered my eyes, as we had been taught to do in air-raid training. Just before I lost consciousness, I had a strange sensation of floating in midair and of being carried by a roaring wind.

When I woke, it was quiet and very dark. Where was I? Was I alive or dead? Though my mind was befuddled, I had enough presence to pinch my cheek. The pain convinced me that I had not died, yet.

But I was surrounded by impenetrable darkness. Trying to stand, I struck my head on something. I touched it. It was concrete. I had been buried. A direct bomb hit had trapped me. Suddenly, I felt death near. Memories flooded my brain. My whole past in an instant. How brief life is.

Just then I perceived a thread of light in the darkness. Red light. It must be from flames. There had been jets of gas flame at intervals of about twelve feet in the factory. They must have ignited some oil. In the dim light, I saw that I was trapped in a narrow space between an iron torpedo-molding plate and part of the collapsed ceiling. The fire seemed to be spreading fast. My little space started filling with smoke. It was difficult to breathe. I suddenly realized that I would die if I did not escape at once. I was seized by a passionate desire to go on living.

Like a trapped rat, I scurried and crawled around the little space in search of a way out. Not a crack anywhere. I pressed my shoulder against the molding plate, but it would not budge. Sitting cross-legged on the floor, I almost gave up hope.

But hope does not die easily. The molding plate would not move, but what about the concrete ceiling? I looked. It was cracked. Then there flashed in my mind the recollection of having stumbled on an iron bar in my scurrying to and fro. I searched and found it, a fairly large screw auger. My last chance. I began

220

jabbing and stabbing at the crack in the concrete with all my strength and desperation.

For what seemed like hours, I worked frantically at the task. At last, I had made a hole large enough for me to crawl through. Later, some time after I had freed myself, I at last saw that my hands were bloody and blistered. I could not use them normally for more than a week.

I had been trapped under the mold for hours. Once free, I was appalled at what I saw. The factory compound was a sea of flames. I heard cries and groans from all directions. One of my fellow workers was pinned between warped posts on the second floor. He called for help. Beside him was a dead body skewered on a piece of iron framework.

More cries of pain, this time from below. I saw two women and a man pinned under a large working table. Putting my shoulder to the edge of the table, I tried to move it. But I could not. The cries subsided; two of the three had already died.

The flames had reached me. My clothes had been either burned or torn; I was naked from the waist up. Unable to do anything for the last of the three people trapped under the table, I dashed for refuge from the fire. My mind was dazed, and I have only the vaguest recollections of what I did next. Little more than half conscious, I ran and ran, through horribly hot air charged with screams and pleas for help. I felt someone briefly pulling my hand.

When I fully regained consciousness, I was in an air-raid shelter beneath the Shotoku-ji temple, more than a hundred meters from the factory compound. A woman was nursing my wounds and cooling my chest with muddy water. She said my chest was badly hurt. My right shoulder had been ripped open so that the bones of the joint were bared. It must have happened when I was blown about by the first blast.

Before long, the smoke and heat in the shelter forced me to go outside. But the combination of the all-enveloping flames and the summer sun was intolerable. I hurried to a nearby muddy stream, took off my trousers, dipped them in the turbid water, and used them to cover my chest and shoulders. I decided that walking up-stream was the only way to safety. On my way, I saw the Zenza Primary School. Jets of flame were spurting from its windows.

Somehow I had escaped to join throngs of refugees fleeing in the direction of Mount Kompira. Having barely escaped death, we walked in stunned, dazed silence. We heard the roar of circling planes overhead. At one point, we encountered Japanese soldiers leading four American prisoners of war. The winners, blue-eyed and laughing, were being scolded by their pathetic Japanese captors. At the top of a hill, we saw the entire Urakami Valley in flames. Black smoke spiraled upward from the raging fires.

With no realization of where I was or where I was going, I simply followed the others. Suddenly I was surprised to see that we had come as far as Hotarujaya. There an old lady, whom I had never met before, took pity on me. She bandaged my bleeding shoulder and gave me sandals to wear, saying it was dangerous to go barefoot, as I had been. Asking where I lived and learning that I came from Yagami, she told me of trucks running in that direction and directed me to the truck stop. But when I got there I found the line of people waiting so long that I decided to walk home.

I suppose it was the old woman's inquiry that suggested going home as fast as possible. I walked a lot that day. Although I saw many abandoned bicycles, I was too confused and muddled to think of taking one. When I reached my neighborhood, people who knew me stared in incredulity. I was so disfigured by my wounds and by blood and dirt that they did not recognize me.

My brothers and sisters were relieved that I was alive and shocked at my condition. I craved water, but my poisoned body would not retain it. I vomited something streaked with a yellowish substance. The mirror showed me a blackened face with white eyes and teeth. My mother, returning from a search for me, was both relieved and shocked by the sight of me. I was taken at once to a nearby hospital for treatment.

That night, I could not sleep. I spent the whole night telling my family of my experiences. My room opened on a highway along which traveled a seemingly endless procession of refugees fleeing the destroyed city, horrifying testimony of the destructive power of the bomb.

On August 15, the emperor shocked the nation by making a radio announcement of surrender. Until then, we had all been convinced that ultimately Japan would be victorious.

In September, one of the workers in our factory called on me with the disturbing news that I had been listed among the dead. On the following day, leaning on a walking stick, I went with him to the shattered wasteland that had been our place of work to clear the matter up. We passed through streets still littered with corpses, though a month had elapsed since the bombing.

When I told the man in charge of our department that I was actually alive, he refused to believe me. I was second from the top on the list of casualties. My wounds had so altered my appearance that he could not recognize me. Many of the people killed in the fire in the plant had been so charred that identification had been impossible. After a few moments, my boss went into the next room for a short while. He returned with a box wrapped in white cloth. It bore the inscription "The Remains of Komaichi Taniyama." Proof that I was dead! It was not until one of my fellow workers identified me definitely that my boss would agree to reinstate me. But it was sad place in which to be reinstated. Only skeleton buildings remained. Dead bodies and ox and horse carcasses lay putrefying on the ground and poisoning the air with a horrid stench. Corpses floated in the waters of the nearby river or lay sprawled on its banks.

Three months later, my gums began to bleed, my hair fell out in tufts, and purplish spots developed all over my body. I suffered from anemia and apathy. I did not regain moderately good health until 1957. Since that time, the symptoms of radiation sickness have not recurred. But one purple spot has persisted on my right arm. It refuses to disappear, as if it were a symbol of the horror of the bomb and a reminder that we must never allow a tragedy like that of Nagasaki to occur again.

A Family
That Experienced Both
Tsugiya Umebayashi

BECAUSE OF THE increasing air raids in 1944, schoolchildren were evacuated from Hiroshima. All of us—I was ten and in the fourth year of primary school—except children of parents living in the outskirts of the city were sent to a Buddhist temple not far away. Life in the group was dull. We did very little. I was lonely. The thing that I remember most vividly is taking off my shirt one sunny Sunday morning to find it infested with lice, which I spent time in crushing. My parents remained in Hiroshima, but in my letters to them I could not complain of loneliness, since our teachers censored our mail. But my parents sent me gifts from time to time. They were my sole source of enjoyment.

Several months after we were evacuated, I traveled to Nagasaki to be with my grandmother, who lived alone and who had asked my parents to send one of the children to live with her.

On the morning of August 9, 1945, I was playing in a stream near an air-raid shelter built by the neighborhood association. Suddenly a flash cut through the sunny sky. I dashed into the shelter. In that same instant, there was a tremendous roar that sounded as if the world were splitting apart. Earth and sand fell over me. For a long time, I waited in fear. Then I felt my head,

224

face, and legs and saw that though covered with dirt I was uninjured.

Hearing voices, I timidly crept out of the shelter to see a sky
filled with billowing black smoke. Over the city, pillars of flame
shot up in many places and spread rapidly. I raced homeward
among destroyed houses and along streets littered with broken
tiles and shattered glass. The hills surrounding it had partly pro-
tected grandmother's house; and when I got there, she was at the
door, about to go looking for me.

On the next day we learned that the kind of bomb that had
fallen on Nagasaki had been dropped on Hiroshima a few days
earlier. There was no way for us to get in touch with my parents
and brothers and sisters. Our anxiety about them mounted steadily.

Finally, unable to remain idle at home any longer, we decided
that, since they had no other place to go, my family would probably evacuate to Nagasaki. To be on hand to meet them and help
them, we went every day to wait at Nagasaki Station.

At first, we had difficulty finding our way. All the old familiar landmarks had been wiped out. The devastation grew worse
toward the Ohato and Dejima areas. Streetcars, wrecked and
burned, stood in the middle of the road. Refugees with tattered,
bloody clothes wandered about aimlessly, looking for relatives
and loved ones. A group of people from the country stood dazed
in front of the ruins of a house where they had expected to find
someone.

The Nagasaki Station area was totally wasted. The only things
still standing were the steel frames of some buildings, bent and
twisted like noodles.

The station officials told us that repairs were under way but
that the prospect of reopening train service was dim and that what
trains ran stopped at Michino Station. Nonetheless, we waited
patiently for hours on end, hoping that our family would be
among the streams of refugees walking along the tracks. As we

waited we saw rescue teams carrying corpses and cremating them on pyres made from the broken posts and beams of destroyed buildings on the station plaza.

On August 14, the repeated trips back and forth to the station began taking their toll on my grandmother's health. Since she was running a fever, we stayed at home that day and the next. Then, on the afternooon of August 15, my parents, my younger brother, and my three younger sisters arrived. They were exhausted and tattered. They carried nothing, since they had been unable to salvage any of our belongings from our destroyed house. Still, we were overjoyed to see them.

When the bomb had fallen on Hiroshima, everyone in our house was trapped under the wreckage. Fortunately, father had not gone to work yet. He extricated himself and then rescued the others. A beam falling on his back seriously injured my younger brother, but all the other members of the family suffered only minor injuries. They left Miyajima, just outside Hiroshima, on August 11; it took them four days to reach Michino Station, from which they picked their way laboriously to grandmother's house. They had to carry my younger brother.

We decided at once to evacuate to Shimabara, our family home town, about forty kilometers east of Nagasaki. After a number of days' waiting, we managed to take a train from Michino Station.

The coach was packed with wounded refugees. The air was foul with the stench of rotting flesh. Flies buzzed everywhere and defeated all attempts to brush them away from wounds, in many of which maggots already wriggled. Some refugees coughed blood into the wash basin. Others had hairless heads. It was impossible to tell whether some of them were men or women.

After a while, we settled down in Shimabara. But my father returned to Hiroshima to work with his old firm. My brother suffered from caries of the spine temporarily, but his symptoms ultimately disappeared. Today he is only slightly incapacitated.

226

The Miracle of Loving Care

Etsuko Fujimura

ON AUGUST 9, 1945, I was at my desk on the second floor of
the Mitsubishi Arms Plant at Ohashi, in Nagasaki. I worked
there as a clerk. We had just returned from the air-raid shelters to
which we had gone when an alarm had been sounded shortly
before eleven. The alert had been lifted, and I had just sat down
to work on some blueprints. My back was toward the window.

Suddenly, I heard a tremendous explosion. I covered my eyes
and ears as we were taught to do in air-raid training. But the blast
hurled me from my place. When I came to, I was sprawled on the
landing at the head of the stairway. Others had been blown out
the windows of the second story and had been killed in their fall.
I lay stock still, paralyzed with fear for about ten minutes. Then I
shouted for help.

The old man who was in charge of machinery and materials
storage in the basement heard my call and came to me. Since I
was unable to walk, he carried me on his back. We escaped the
ruined and burning building.

I had been badly hurt. The part of my face that I had covered
with my hands had been spared to an extent, but my forehead
was mangled and bleeding. When I lowered my head, the skin of
my forehead hung down in front of my eyes like a piece of tattered cloth. Part of my clothing had been blown off, and my back
was brutally wounded. Ashamed of my nakedness, after we had
gone a little way I asked the old man to put me down in a paddy.
Since he was returning to the factory, I asked him to tell my
father, who was the director of the propulsion department, where
to find me. Before long, I heard someone call my name. To my
intense happiness, it was my father, who had happened to meet
the old man. Because of my serious condition he insisted that I go

227

at once to the safety of the country. My mother, sister, and younger brother had evacuated to Yue; but ironically they had all three returned on an errand to our home in the Iwakawa-machi district of Nagasaki. My father intended to go to look for them. I was frightened and did not want to part from him, but at about three in the afternoon it became necessary for us to go our separate ways. He promised to join me in the country as soon as he had found the others.

On my way to Michino, where I wanted to take a freight train, I happened to meet a close friend who had worked at the same factory. She begged me to take her with me. We started off together, only to find our path blocked by the carcass of a dead horse. Though terrified, we decided that we had to pull ourselves together and survive somehow.

Just then, a weak but frenzied voice called our names and pleaded for help. We rushed to the place from which the voice came and found another friend, dying from a ghastly rip in the chest. There was nothing we could do for her. Though it tormented us, we had to abandon her with nothing but the faint hope that someone would come soon and take her to a hospital.

American planes circling overhead were dropping incendiary bombs. Our progress was so slow that it was about seven in the evening when we finally reached the station and got on the freight train, filled with horribly wounded people. Some of them had attacks of diarrhea in the car.

My friend got off at Isahaya, but I went on to Omura, where there was a hospital. I realized that I required medical attention fast and hoped to be treated before continuing to the country. A member of a relief team took me to the Kyosai Hospital in Omura, where I was bandaged from head to foot and ordered to remain absolutely still.

But the next day, the city of Omura underwent another of the bomb raids that I was told had become daily. Buildings near the hospital were in flames. Not knowing when our turn might come and not wanting to be killed there, I decided to go on to the country, where others of my brothers and sisters were living. As luck would have it, I met an acquaintance from the country who wanted to leave the hospital too. Covered with bandages, the two of us sneaked out of the ward and went to the station. Since we had no money, we resolved to walk. But before long this became too tiring; and we returned to the station, where the officials took pity on our condition and gave us a free ride.

At about ten in the evening, I reached Yue and went to the house where my sisters lived. At first appalled by my appearance, they soon wept for joy that I was alive. They had heard about the bombing of Nagasaki.

Presently my father returned, alone. He had gone to the place where our house had stood and had found nothing but rubble. He looked for a while but found nothing. About to leave, he ran into a neighbor who said she had seen mother the minute before the blast. The neighbor had been entering the air-raid shelter when mother said she and the children would be along at once. Feeling that mother could not have gone far, father began to dig in the smoldering ruins of our house. He found mother, one of my sisters, and my brother dead, buried under the wreckage. He had the bodies cremated and brought the remains, including mother's false teeth, back with him in a rice cooker that we had used for many years.

From that day, my temperature shot up to between forty and forty-two degrees centigrade. I was in a delirium for days. Having heard from someone that falling hair and purple spots on the skin were major symptoms of the dreaded atomic disease, my sisters felt reassured. I had neither of the symptoms. But in a few days they developed. My hair fell, and purple spots appeared on several parts of my body.

The first hospital I visited said that there was nothing to be done, implying that I was doomed to die. But I went to another hospital, where a woman doctor named Ushijima examined me. Looking intently into my face, she said that I had the atomic disease and that she could make no promises. But she added that she had no intention of remaining idle while young people like me were suffering from this horrible sickness. Insisting that I remain quiet and follow her instructions, she initiated treatment.

But my fever did not go down, my gums bled, and my hair continued to fall. I had no appetite and ate virtually nothing. Dr. Ushijima, who was so attentive that she would come even at midnight if I showed signs of getting worse, gave me frequent dextrose injections and performed operations on festering sores on my neck. I drank a concoction made of boiled persimmon leaves and ate ground radish without any signs of improvement in my condition.

At one juncture, death seemed very close. My father asked if there was anything I would like to eat, and I replied that I would be able to die content if they would give me a pear. Two of my sisters immediately went out to purchase the fruit and on the way met a nun who seemed to know a great deal about radiation sickness. Apparently she had taken care of many atomic-bomb victims. When my sisters told her about me, she said there was a remedy that would work in my case.

"I think I can save your sister. Victims of the atomic sickness die because their stomachs and intestines are filled with poisonous gas. The most important thing is to get the gas out of their systems. Go to a village about two miles from here. At the drugstore specializing in Chinese remedies there ask for Tentokosan. If your sister's stool is bloody after taking this medicine, she will survive. If not, there is no hope for her."

My sisters bought the medicine at once. I took it and almost immediately felt my bowels become loose. Getting out of bed and starting for the toilet, I fainted. My sisters, who heard my fall, rushed from the kitchen to help me. I was later told that I passed two bucketfuls of bloody fecal matter.

Then, fifty days after the bombing, I experienced my second major crisis. I lost consciousness and once again lingered on the brink of death. My father and sisters and Dr. Ushijima gathered at my bedside. Before long, however, I regained consciousness and could see blurred faces around me. I had apparently pulled through. Dr. Ushijima examined me and said that I would live.

My condition improved rapidly. In a few days, my temerature fell; and ten days later the purple spots were completely gone. Miraculously, I was cured and I have never suffered a relapse or any aftereffects. Doctors and experts on the subject tell me that I am one of the few people who were within a radius of one and a half kilometers of the hypocenter who are still alive and healthy today. Nonetheless, the Atomic Bomb Casualty Commission sends officials to examine me regularly twice a year; and all my records are kept at the Nagasaki University Hospital.

Perhaps the Chinese herbal medicine helped cure me; I cannot say. But I am certain that the patient and loving care of my family and of Dr. Ushijima are largely responsible for the good health I enjoy today.

Glass Reminders
Masako Okawa

AS IF FROM FAR AWAY, the faint voice of my mother called, "Masako! Masako! Where are you?"

Where was I? What had happened to me? My head throbbed heavily. Pain first stabbed then suddenly stopped, leaving me as light as a feather. My head did not seem to be my own. I was crammed into a tiny black space, all alone. Something dripped from my head.

Once again, I heard my mother's weak voice. This time, I answered, "Mother, I'm here. Where are you?"

"Thank heaven, you're alive. Are you hurt?"

231

"It's so dark here, and I can't move."

After a while, I raised my hand to my head. Then a ray of light filtered in from somewhere. Frantically I pushed aside dirt, boards, roofing tiles, and other debris, finally extricating myself. Sudden bright sunlight after the darkness of my prison shocked my eyes.

Still more shocking was what I beheld. Our house had collapsed. As far as I could see, only the ferroconcrete Nagasaki Medical College was still standing; and flames were pouring from its windows.

I was a child of eight on August 9, 1945, when the atom bomb was dropped on Nagasaki.

Mother and my two younger sisters were still buried under the wreckage that had been our house. "I'm out!" I shouted. My mother heard me and asked how I was. For the first time since breaking free, I examined myself. The raw flesh of my arms was exposed. Something hung over one of my ears. I tried to push it away. It was a piece of my scalp. A big gash ran from above my left eye to the top of my head, and the substance that had been dripping over me was my own blood. My face, abdomen, and legs were covered with cuts. I found movement difficult. The only thing I could do was whimper to my mother for help.

Finally she and my sisters were pulled from the heap of debris. As we hurried to the open space of a cemetery for foreigners, we heard piteous pleas for help from the burning wreckage around us. But everyone who could was fleeing and paid no heed.

Heaps of dead and injured filled the cemetery. People who remained alive cried out in anguish for water. At stagnant, blood-covered pools, human beings swarmed like ants around sugar. No matter how foul, the water was welcome to victims of the atom bomb.

My grandmother used to frighten me with stories of the flames and tormenting needles that I would suffer in hell if I were not good. But I had tried to be good, and yet I was being forced to endure the pain of hell while still alive. What had the good

232

woman next door done to deserve being trapped in the flaming wreck of her house. What had any of us done?

After our night of trying to sleep on the bare ground, someone from my mother's home village of Miemura found us and led us back with him. Everyone who saw me said I would be lucky to live another day. I was the only one of the four of us to survive.

Though she suffered only an injury in the leg, a month later, my mother died, mad. One after another, my two small sisters, apparently uninjured, followed her.

Though I grew stronger, I was disfigured. All the hair had fallen from my head, and children embarrassed me horribly with taunting cries of "Baldy! Baldy!"

In March of the following year, my soldier father, repatriated from Taiwan, returned to Nagasaki and remarried. But my hopes for a new, peaceful existence were to be frustrated by the battle for life ordained for all victims of the atomic diseases, which killed thousands and doomed thousands more to limitless days in sickbeds and hopelessness. At first, I seemed completely healthy, but I could never be sure I was safe.

The shame of my disfigurement tormented me constantly. Scores of tiny fragments of glass picked from my face had left visible scars. These and other scars turned blue-black, like tattoos. The gash extending from above my left eye to the top of my head healed by forming a grotesque lump of flesh. My classmates jeered and called me "a mess" and "a monster." Some people laughed when they passed me on the streets. Others were kinder and asked me why I did not wash the ink off my face. I repeatedly put to myself the question, "What have I done to warrant this punishment?" Like other women, I wanted to be pretty and admired. The sight that greeted me in the mirror offered no consolation in my misery.

After graduating from junior high school, I began to notice the appearance of symptoms of the dread atomic disease: periodic nausea, low blood pressure, hypersensitivity to cold, internal hemorrhage, and purple spots on my arms and legs. Though the

233

spots disappeared, they usually returned in a few days to inspire me with horror of the day when my entire body would be covered with them and I would die.

Ostensibly dedicated to the welfare of humanity, but perverted by wicked leaders, science and technology created the atomic bomb. Today, in spite of their sophistication, science and technology continue to fail to evolve a cure for the diseases caused by atom-bomb radiation. The splinters of glass still embedded in the flesh of my arms are tiny witnesses to the tragedy resulting from the perversion of human knowledge.

The Danger Today

Later in that house
fire suddenly broke out,
in one moment on four sides
its flames raging everywhere.
Beams, rafters, joists, pillars
with crackling sounds trembled and split,
broke in two, came tumbling down;
walls and partitions toppled and fell.

. . .

At that time the master of the house,
standing outside the gate,
heard someone say,
"All your children
a while ago, in the midst of play,
came and entered this house.
They are young and lack understanding,
lost in enjoyment, amusement, and sport."

. . .

But the children lacked understanding.
Though they heard their father's warnings,
still they remained lost in enjoyment,
never ceasing their games and play.

LOTUS SUTRA, Chapter 3